We Are Absolutely Not Okay

Fourteen Stories by Teenagers Who Are Picking Up the Pieces

By

Amelia Dawn Dahlen
Tebra Draper
Miranda Esau
Jeanette Figueroa
Jasmine Gifford
Leandra Hall
Kayla Kinnard
Bre Klein
Lauren Nein
Charlie Magdalena
C. Jordan "Rivers" Meador
Stephanie Tangedahl
Neal Tingley
Fabian Vazquez

Note: For privacy reasons, some names have been changed

Edited/Compiled by Marjie Bowker & Ingrid Ricks

Proofreading by Carol Bowker & Sarah Philley

We Are Absolutely Not Okay
Fourteen Stories by Teenagers Who Are Picking Up the Pieces

Copyright © 2012
by Edmonds School District

ISBN: 978-0-615-63860-7

All RIGHTS RESERVED

Cover Design by: Carolina Mooney & Bre Klein

Edited and compiled by Marjie Bowker and Ingrid Ricks

Print book formatting by Hydra House

Published by Scriber Lake High School

TABLE OF CONTENTS

OUR INTENTION WITH THIS STORY COLLECTION

IF YOU HAVE EVER FELT ALONE, betrayed, confused or angry, this book is for you. If you have ever come to school pretending everything is okay when really everything is absolutely not, we want you to know that there is hope—even in the darkest situations. We are real and our stories are real, so you need not feel alone with your struggles.

It is not easy to write about depression, abuse, self-harm or sexual identity; however, writing has become our outlet to cope with the past and our doorway to seize the future. We challenged ourselves to find our voices and to write our truths. We hope that you will connect with our stories and find the strength to walk with confidence into the future with us.

❀

A Note from Scriber Lake High School Principal Kathy Clift

I find that people often judge students like ours unfairly. Many students come to an alternative school because they don't fit into the comprehensive high schools and need a much smaller environment where they can become successful. Scriber students are often said to be "at-risk children." As I have come to know them, I am convinced that they are "children of promise" who just need a safe place to continue the hard work they have already begun. They are resilient enough to show up and move forward. I hope their stories build a bridge to more understanding and dialogue.

RUN UP OR SHUT UP

FABIAN VAZQUEZ

"DON'T BE SCARED," my homeboy told me.

I was shaking. Sweat was building between the palm of my hand and the handle of the single action .22 revolver I was holding. I had never held a gun and, being the size that I was, I thought it was really heavy. I felt the pressure in my head, imagining how it could all go wrong. It seemed like the whole world knew what I was about to do and the glares of the few people that walked past terrified me. But I couldn't show any type of weakness. I had to make it seem like I was in control of the situation.

I had received the call that would place me here a couple of days before from one of my homeboys.

"What's good, little homie?" he had said over my cell phone's speakerphone. His ranking was a "Soldier," meaning he was one of many roots that held the gang in place. He had been in the clique since it started.

"Nothing," I replied with a rough voice, trying to act tough.

"You down to put in work this weekend? Because there is a meeting set up and your cousin talked about you coming in. It's now or never little homie," he said in a voice that made my heart pump faster.

"Yeah," I mumbled, not wanting to hear or see what was coming next.

"Is he going to be there?"

My cousin had been in the gang for a couple months before I joined in and he was already ranked as "Third Word" in the gang, meaning that his words counted when the gang made a decision. We had moved from Mexico City two years earlier when I was ten. Neither of us had known anyone, and we couldn't speak to anyone. The transition was difficult, but through the gang he had found a family who understood what we were going through. As a result, they were quickly becoming my family too and I wanted in.

"Na, he says it's your decision and you're on your own. But don't worry. Ain't nothing out of the ordinary. We just going hunting, trying to get some cash. You up for it?" he asked.

"Alright then, I'm down," I said firmly. A feeling of desperation washed over me.

I had just given my word and I couldn't let them down.

"Cool, I'll be seeing you little one," he said, and then hung up.

After that call my mind had just two thoughts, to rob or to leave and never step up. If I didn't do this I would never be able to join the gang.

A couple of days later, I was mobbing through the streets of downtown Everett with three other members and a gun, looking for a mark.

"All you got to do is point and ask for everything. If they don't give it up you just take it," one of my homeboys instructed me.

I didn't answer. I knew what I had to do. If it all went bad and the police found me or caught me in the act, I knew I had to keep my mouth shut. We kept walking and my homeboy passed me a joint. "This will keep you calm," he told me.

I didn't hesitate to take a couple hits. "It's the good shit," I said.

I slowly drifted into the clouds and wished I could keep getting high, but I felt nervous so I knew my high wouldn't last long. We walked through a parking lot and saw a middle-aged woman stepping out of a grey metallic Lexus that was sitting on some fresh wheels.

"You ready?" my homeboy asked.

I nodded and started trailing the woman. My homies stayed behind. I felt scared, my heart pounded to the rhythm of her steps. She was wearing all black: heels, leggings, skirt and a blouse. She looked like a grumpy old lady that was never pleased about anything in her life. This fueled my anger, as if she had done something that enraged me to commit some sort of revenge on her. Horrifying thoughts filled my head, like shooting her accidentally and going to prison for half of my life. My body temperature dropped. I felt myself shaking more than ever.

Then I felt the demons, like shadows, slowly enter my body. They were filled with evil and were looking for a victim who was confused and lonely. I heard a voice in my head that spoke to me in a slow, angry voice. "If you do this, your lifestyle will be better," it rasped.

"How much better will it be?" I asked.

"I'll make your lifestyle even better than you can imagine or dream of," it answered.

I came back to the present and realized I was right behind the woman. I looked around to make sure I didn't spot anyone.

This is it. Fuck it! I said to myself. I took a deep breath and swallowed. "Hey!" I yelled.

As she turned around, I grabbed her and threw her against the wall. She tried screaming but I put the gun to her head and whispered, "I'm going to make it easy. Give me all you got and I won't have to blow your head off!" I yelled at the end, but I wasn't worried about that. I just wanted her to act quickly before this turned into something I would regret.

She froze. She looked surprised and shocked. I could see fear in her shiny blue eyes, but they looked at me with such power that I almost ran away. She didn't say a word. I felt like crying. The evil thoughts in my head pushed the fear back inside me.

The woman was shaking. I let go and snatched her purse away, still pointing the gun at her head. I quickly fumbled through all of the items in her purse with my other hand to make sure her cell phone was in there. It would have been a red flag for me if I left the scene without that cell phone. Even I knew that.

"Don't say shit!" was the last thing I said to her. She gave me one last glance filled with disgust before I took off and ran. As soon as my homeboys spotted me they booked it, too. I followed them, running through the back streets. I watched them jump into a red Honda Civic that pulled up in front of them from out of nowhere. For a moment I thought they were going to leave me there, but then the Honda pulled up next to me and I got in. I exhaled in relief, sat back, and then said to my homeboys, "I need a cigarette." I didn't smoke cigarettes, but at that moment the adrenaline was rushing through my body and I needed to have one.

I took the pack I was handed and began combing through the woman's purse while we sped away. I became irritated because there were so many things inside. The purse was cluttered with makeup, keys, tissues, a mirror and other useless things.

"Fuck, there's hella shit inside this thing!" I said in a loud voice. I was relieved to be done with the job, but now I worried that I hadn't come through for my homies. There had to be something good in there.

My homies patted me on the back. Not one of them seemed concerned about whether I had actually scored anything worthwhile. "That's what's up little homie," they said. "You really down for this shit, huh!"

I finally spotted her wallet. I opened it and found close to five hundred dollars.

"We about to party tonight," I said in a happy tone, feeling no remorse whatsoever.

I don't know if it was the money that made me feel good or the fact that the whole thing was over. Either way, this was the new lifestyle I had chosen, and from then on I was a regular criminal. I had crossed the threshold and now considered myself a menace to society.

❧

A Note About Fabian Vazquez

Fabian Vazquez is a junior at Scriber Lake High School. He was born and raised in Mexico City with his younger sister. He came to the U.S when he was just ten years old and has been living in the Shoreline area since then. Fabian is a very smart, intelligent young man who has been able to succeed in life with the help of his parents and teachers, as well as other influences.

He has gone through a rough past living in poverty in his country and tried to fit in with the wrong crowd when he came to the U.S. Fabian got out of a gang before it was too late and his main hope now is to let other teens know that gangs are "no way out" and that they are "the road to no success."

He is now a 4.0 student and is always on track with his schoolwork. He holds the record at his school for sit-ups (1001 in one session). He has received awards for many subjects including English, math, art and science. He was also selected for the Edmonds Exchange Club "Accepting the Challenge of Excellence" Award. Fabian definitely wants to go to college and would like to do something related to arts or architecture.

A TASTE OF THE REAL WORLD

LEANDRA HALL

"OH COME ON, BABY. I just wanna spend some time with you." The man's deep, low voice sent shivers down my spine. The feeling of his hand rubbing my upper back kept me frozen in fear. "How much will it take?"

A day that had started just like any other turned out to be one I'd remember for years to come. Aside from my uncle visiting from California, it was a typical day at home. There was some yelling and fighting, with things thrown across rooms. I was thirteen years old, and the way I saw it, if *anyone* tried to take authority over me, they were automatically an enemy. I was going to do drugs, have sex, run away and whatever else I felt like doing and no one but me was allowed to control it.

I didn't know my uncle very well. Since he lived so far away, we'd only met a few times. Of course, he tried to lecture me about something and we got into an argument. I put on a jacket, grabbed my skateboard, and was on my way out of the house. My parents didn't know where I was going. In fact, I didn't really know where I was going.

I acted without thinking. I skateboarded down the street to the 101 bus stop on the highway that would bring me northbound, toward Everett. Along the way I devised a plan that involved picking up a few friends who always hung out at the bus station, then taking the hour-and-a-half long commuter bus ride all the way to Seattle. We could go to my first rave. This was exciting because I had tried to go to at least five raves and had never actually made it.

It took two buses to get from my house to the Everett station. There was a point on the main road where I had to get off the 101 and transfer to the 9. This is where I met *him*.

I stood at the bus stop along with about six other people. They were all responsible-looking adults who gave me funny looks when I first walked up. I stared impatiently at the intersection where the 9 was to turn left to pick us up. The highway was busy as usual for a Friday afternoon, with what seemed like hundreds of cars passing each minute.

Finally, I saw the bus; it was ten minutes late. Those last few seconds of waiting seemed to drag on for minutes. As I waited for the other people to get on and pay their fares, a black man wearing a white turban and dark clothes stepped off the bus. At first I didn't pay much attention to him.

"I like your skateboard," he said from behind me.

"Oh, thanks ... " I mumbled shyly after turning around to see who was talking.

"You smoke?" he asked.

"Cigarettes?" At this point, I actually faced him and got a good look at him. The sclera of his eyes was as yellow as his teeth, as if he had jaundice. He looked old, at least in his mid-thirties. He was relatively skinny, but he was still a lot bigger and taller than me. Altogether, he was about twice my size.

"Yes," he said, smiling back at me with those horrid yellow teeth.

"Yeeeah ... ?" I said in a questioning tone, since I didn't understand why he was asking.

"Want me to buy you a pack?"

His offer really caught me off guard. People don't usually ask thirteen-year-olds if they want a pack; it's usually the other way around. I was a little suspicious about why he would go out of his way to offer that.

"I don't have any money," I said, trying to get him off my back. I started walking toward the door of the bus.

"I'll buy 'em for you!" he called after me, sounding desperate to keep me off the bus.

I stopped. *Why not?* I reasoned with myself. *It's a free pack of cigarettes. I can just wait for the next bus and I'll have cigarettes to smoke to take up some time.* I knew deep down that he had intentions other than just "helping out" some kid, but I pushed that thought aside.

I turned to face him. "Okay," I said, then proceeded to look around for the nearest convenience store. I pointed out the Chevron only about a half a block away, on the same side of the street. As we walked he asked me some basic questions like "What's your name?" and "Where are you going?" These questions were seriously boring the hell out of me.

"What kind do you want?" he asked me once we got within twenty feet of the convenience store's main entrance.

"Marb Menthol Light 100s."

"I'll be right back," he replied. I carefully stood out of the cashier's sight through the window, within a few feet of the side of the building. Once again, I played the waiting game. I had nothing to do but to think, and nothing to think about except how much I wanted to hurry up and leave so I could get to that rave. I also thought about how this guy was a little creepy and if I didn't get away from him soon, he could try to rape me or something else that might happen in a movie. I wasn't scared though. I figured that I was grown and could take care of myself.

He finally emerged from the store with the cigarettes and a white plastic bag carrying two silver cans. He handed me a small white- and green-colored box filled with twenty sticks of tobacco and cotton, wrapped in the same colored paper. I quickly opened them and started to smoke one.

"Do you smoke weed?" he asked.

"Yeah."

"Wanna come to my apartment and smoke a bowl?" he continued. "I just live about a block away."

At this point I was certain he was up to something, but I was stupid and naïve. I was a wanna-be rebel trying to live on the edge. So, in my insanity, I decided to go with him.

After walking farther down the highway for two or three minutes, he veered to the right, off of the sidewalk, onto a driveway which quickly ended with a black barred gate a few inches taller than me. It had sharp points at the end of the bars on the top. Once we reached the gate, he typed a code into a keypad housed on the left side of the gate, next to where it opened.

For a moment I wondered how I was going to get out of the complex when I left. In my mind, I pictured him walking me all the way back to the end of the parking lot to open the gate. I quickly decided that was unlikely.

Through the gate I could see a complex of tan and light brown three-story apartment buildings. We entered the complex and started up the stairs of the third building from the entrance. Once we reached the second floor, he stopped at a door and unlocked it with a set of keys from his pocket.

My first thought when I walked into his apartment was to question the emptiness. This one bedroom apartment had nothing in it but a few dishes in the kitchen and a mattress with two sheets lying on the living room floor. He had me take off my shoes, so I threw them next to my skateboard. He walked out onto the porch. When I stepped outside, he was smoking the weed with a pipe made out of duct tape, which I had never seen. We passed the pot back and forth until it was out and my vision started to blur like the vision in a dream. I got really tired and lethargic, but that was normal for me. My body was shaky and I felt uncomfortable. We went back inside.

"You want a beer?" he asked, pulling one of the silver cans out of his bag.

"Sure," I said, and took it out of his hand. I examined the can since I hadn't recognized the purple "211" writing on it or the name "Steel Reserve." I opened it and took a sip of the worst tasting drink in the world. I sat on the mattress and forced myself to keep drinking it.

After another few minutes, I checked the time on my phone and realized it'd been over an hour since he stopped me from getting on the bus. I got a little nervous, worried that I might not be able to get to the station in time to catch my friends.

"Oh wow. I should really get going. It's been a really long time," I said. I got up, sat the beer on the counter, and made my way toward the front door.

"Wait, stay a little longer and spend some time with me!" he practically begged.

"No. I should really go," I quickly responded, concerned about why he sounded so desperate for me to stay.

"Well, do you have any money?"

"No, but that's okay. I can get some from my friends," I said, even though I really wanted him to give me money. I just knew he wouldn't give me money for free. I continued walking toward the door.

"How much do you need? I can give it to you."

"I only need twenty-five dollars but that's okay, you don't need to give me any money," I said while putting on my shoes.

He walked over to me and asked for a hug.

After getting my shoes all of the way on, I tried to give him a quick hug, but he started to beg me to stay and "spend time with him." I knew what he really meant —he wanted me to have sex with him. I was shaking uncontrollably. My heart pounded, my body went numb, and I thought I might pass out. He gripped me tighter and started rubbing his hands on my back. He continued to beg.

"I'll give you twenty-five dollars; I'll give you forty, eighty, a hundred dollars."

"No!" I screamed and, almost out of nowhere, I followed the urge of my instincts telling me to act. With adrenaline pumping, I pushed him off me. I guess his grip wasn't as tight as it felt, because I almost made him fall.

I grabbed my skateboard and slammed the door behind me, running down the stairs as fast as I could. I just ran without even thinking about it. When I got to the gate, I didn't even bother to give myself time to figure out how to get it open. I just threw my skateboard over and started climbing, squeezing my feet between the bars. Once I reached the ground, I jumped on my skateboard and moved as quickly as I could, back to the 101 bus stop.

I got to the bus stop and sat for a moment. Then I decided to lie down. It was getting dark, and I was cold and scared. I just wanted to be home, I didn't even care about the rave anymore. I felt violated because of the way he had touched me and because he had even thought about having sex with me. At home I knew I would be safe and right then it was worth putting up with the dysfunction for safety. For the next fifteen minutes, I cried.

By the time the bus pulled up, I couldn't wait to get home.

A Note From Leandra Hall

Today, I'm seventeen. After some other experiences in my life, I don't run away anymore and I'm clean and sober. This story was one of many events that taught me to appreciate my family—my mom, my dad, and my four sisters. I take full responsibility for the mistakes I've made but I don't beat myself up for those or my imperfections because I learn and grow from them. I was lucky to have gotten away so easily and it took me a long time to realize it. This story is for any teen who thinks breaking the rules is necessary to have fun. I never saw that man again and I'll leave it at that.

BASTARD CHILD

C. JORDAN "RIVERS" MEADOR

I CUT DEEP INTO MY SKIN with a sharp, thin blade and wince. I chuckle to myself as a distraction from the stinging in my leg. Tiny little drops of red start appearing through the surface. They flow together and roll off my ankle. I let out a sigh of relief. Thank. Goodness. Another slice follows the first. The hair growing on my legs—more than overdue for a shave —sticks out about a quarter of an inch off my lower leg. I watch as the blood trails around the hairs like a river running through a forest.

Each "cutting session" includes the same routine: I think of one reason or another as to why my self-harm is justified. Thought, cut, thought, cut, thought, cut. *I'm a terrible best friend.* First incision. *I never do anything right.* Second incision. *I'm not good enough.* Third. *I can't believe I slept with him.* Fourth. *Nobody will ever love me.* Fifth. *I should probably just kill myself.* Sixth.

I think up thirty-three reasons and create thirty-three bright red horizontal lines up and down my left lower shin.

Cut.

I think about the night before last. I'm lying in bed with a stranger. His strong, rough hands are running down the small of my back and over my ass. He touches my body in a way that suggests he knows me, that he loves me. But this isn't love—this is a mirage of what love might look like. There's no emotion in this situation. He's following what his penis wants and what he thinks his heart wants. I'm only here because I'm naïve and want to feel loved—I need to feel loved in order to feel alive.

I don't look him in the eye.

"Do it from behind," I say. *Please, don't see how hideous I really am.* I fake the finish so he can have an actual finish. I immediately get up and put my clothes on. I grab my bag and cigarettes and start the hour and a half walk to my house. *I hope my boyfriend doesn't find out about this.*

I make another cut and think back to last week.

I watch a red coffee mug fly over my head and smash against the wall behind me. I duck low to the floor—the cup just barely missing my head—as scalding liquid splatters my shirt. Standing, staring at me from where the mug flew is Renée. Tears run down her face. Her make-up is smeared over her beautiful pale, freckled skin. I can see the hatred burning behind her glossy, blue-grey eyes. I can feel the coldness as she speaks hard and truthful.

"What the fuck?" A common question asked by Renée. "Didn't we just go over this?"

"I know. I'm sorry," I whimper in response.

"He's nothing but unhealthy for you. And he's ruining our friendship."

"I need him, Nay. He—he saved my life."

"I've been here for you for eleven years and then this guy just shows up out of the blue and *he's* the one to save you? Is this a joke?"

"That's not what I mean. You're my best friend. It's just—"

"It's just what, Jordan?"

I don't know how to respond, so I just stare at her sadly.

"That's what I thought. It's him or me. And if you think he's so much more important than me, then fine. I'm done."

I'm so confused and shocked and sad that I can hardly breathe as she turns and walks out the back door of my house.

It's bad enough that I want to put a bullet in my head. For real. Now it feels like my best friend is validating my decision.

Cut.

Another memory flashes through my mind. At least, I think it's a memory. I vaguely remember it happening.

I'm five or six years old. A neighbor boy and I put blankets all around the trampoline to create a fort underneath, concealing the bright summer afternoon. He tells me to take off my pants. Being naïve and a few years younger than he is, I assume we're going to play a game. I do what he tells me. Then he unzips his pants and makes me touch his "private parts" as he touches mine.

I have never thought much about this memory that may or may not be true, but for some reason, it sticks in my mind. I am thinking of it now. I don't know what to make of it. All I know is that it's a good enough reason for me to cut.

As I sit on the sand-colored carpet in my bedroom, I make sure the black towel under my legs will catch any blood that's dripping. I can't let anyone see what I've done. I wonder who would care. I know for a fact my father wouldn't. He abandoned me as a baby, leaving me to be a bastard child so that he could live with his perfect little family. That worthless piece of shit is the reason why I have so many issues. He doesn't care about me at all. If he did, he would have actually wanted to see me. He's never even taken the time to call me. He has not even inquired about me. *He's* the reason why it would be so easy to commit suicide. If my own father doesn't want me, how could anyone else?

I press one last time into my beat-up flesh. I start low on the inside of my ankle, slowly pulling the box knife up toward my knee. There is only one thought running through my head. My vision turns to black. *I hope I don't wake up in a hospital—I hope this time I wake up dead.*

❦

A Note From C. Jordan "Rivers" Meador

Now that I'm eighteen years old, I have not inflicted any self-harm for three years. I am currently in a healthy relationship with a very amazing boy. We have only been together for three months, but we are both perfectly content, and I know I will never ever cheat on him. I've been going to therapy in order to help deal with my past, and I'm learning to forgive myself. I am on my way to "happily ever after."

COMING OUT

BRE KLEIN

I CANNOT BELIEVE it has taken me two months since I came out of the closet to even THINK of telling my dad. I feel like an asshole for telling everyone but him.

"It's time," Grandma says. She's sitting across the room on the couch, leaning forward. A worried look is written across her face. She's one of the first people I came out to as a transgender man, and she is slowly learning more about it as I teach her. "He's going to find out sooner or later. You may as well tell him and get it over with."

"What if he disowns me?" I ask the question aloud to no one in particular, my voice shaking. I'm sitting in my favorite recliner chair, one we've had since I was a small child. I like to rock in it when I'm thinking or upset. It reminds me of better times. "He'll never accept me as his son," I say wearily. My dad had only just recently made his way back into my life, and I wasn't ready to lose him again. He is a changed man from when I was a kid. Our trust was finally building back up. "I'll only ever be his daughter, his sweetie pie, his—"

Grandma interrupts this melodramatic rant with a firm grip of my shoulders. "You're his child," she begins, "and he loves you; he'll always accept you for whatever you choose to do."

A tear pools in the corner of my eye and runs down my cheek. Grandma still has yet to realize that being a transgender person is not a choice. But I ignore her choice of words and give a firm nod. If anyone is to tell him, it's going to be me.

Minutes later I climb into the passenger seat of Dad's green Saturn and give him a hug. It's Friday night, and I'm about to head to his house for visitation. Well, my brother and I never call it 'visitation' anymore; we don't visit him only because it's court-ordered. Actually, it has turned into multiple nights a week at his house for dinner. Something about this little fact makes my heart ache even more in fear of how Dad will react to the news. "Goddammit, my child's an IT!" I imagine him saying.

Of course, I'm not an "it." But I have no idea what Dad will do, and a lot of people think that people like me are, in fact, "its." They have yet to realize I'm just like them, but that my outside just doesn't match what's inside like it does for them.

"Hey, how's it going?" I ask, smiling a bit while I buckle my seatbelt. I start to plan in my head how I want—hope—for this to go. Internally nervous, I look at the street ahead as Dad starts to rev the car's engine. Damn, I should have thought through the delivery of this news a little bit more. How to tell, when to tell, where to tell? ... Why to tell?

"Good, good. The usual," Dad says casually as he quickly shifts gears with the clutch. I hate riding in stick shifts, even if Dad *did* know how to drive them like a pro. I always get anxious, afraid that the gears will give out or something. I quickly fumble through my pockets, feeling for a familiar rectangular package. Finally finding it in one of the six pockets of my army-style jacket, I roll down the window and light a cigarette. I sit back a bit, letting a stream of smoke out of my mouth. I watch it roll out the window. Dad's eyes shift toward me. He knows I only smoke in the car if I'm stressed or anxious.

"Something on your mind, honey?" he asks, lifting a brow. The last word stings hard, making me wince. I hate it when he does that shit. Sure, of course he doesn't know the pain that saying names like that brings. How would he know? He more than likely has no idea about my current situation. But, either way, it still hurts like hell. I ignore the urge to say something. No, not yet. Instead, I shrug and look back out the window.

"No, not really. Just tired," I mutter as another puff of smoke fills my lungs. That's always my excuse for when I'm upset or down, and when I don't want to talk about my feelings. Tiredness. I prefer to bottle it up and ignore it for a while, then deal with it later when I'm alone. I don't like talking about my feelings. My eyes shift a bit as Dad pats my shoulder.

"Yeah, I definitely know how that goes. Just let me know if you wanna talk, sweetie," he says, with a sympathetic smile. Bam. Again my heart is torn a little more with the daughter-only pet names. Using my peripherals, I set my gaze on his face. There's worry in his blue eyes, almost the same shade as mine. I love our eyes, even if sometimes I am a little bit jealous of my brother's deep-chocolate brown eyes inherited from Mom.

"We're going to the store to get stuff for dinner. Want me to drop you off at the apartment first?" he asks as we inch closer to his house. I pause in my response, trying to buy another minute to think. A public place could be a really decent place to tell him. Not a lot of people would think that it would be a good idea, and I don't blame them. Who would want to talk about something so private in front of an audience of strangers?

But they don't know my dad like I do. Not only did I inherit his eyes, I also got a good portion of his anger issues. When we get mad, we get *mad*. A lot of yelling can be, and usually is, involved. If we were in a public place, however, he would have to hold himself back and bottle it all up in silence. That would give me a chance to give a better explanation than just, 'Oh by the way, I'm a dude. Just thought I'd let you know.'

"Nah, I'll go to the store with you. I wanna buy an energy drink anyway," I say with a faint smile.

As the Saturn lurches closer and closer to QFC, I practically start counting every foot the car travels. Time feels like it's slipping through the palms of my hands. Inch by inch we go, and my pulse beats to the point I think my heart's going to burst out of my chest and through the window. How the hell do I do this? Should I just sugarcoat it and lay it on softly? *So, Daddy, I'm not your little girl anymore. In fact, I never really have been. Sorry I didn't tell you.* Or, should I be funny about it? *So Pops, I doubt you like watching birth being given. Guess what? You'll never have to see your son go into labor unless, by some magical science, men can start having babies.* No, no. He has a (kind of lame) sense of humor, but this was a bit too serious of a situation to be pulling that shit. In that case, should I be straightforward and blunt?

"Dad, I'm a transgender ... guy," I say aloud, accidentally using my outside-voice from all the anxiety building up in my system. I'm quickly taken aback by what the hell just slipped out of my big, fat mouth. No, I wasn't ready! Oh no, no ... My eyes are wide as I sink down into my seat, wanting to melt and dissolve into the fabric. I would kill to be anywhere but here. Regret, regret! I wasn't ready to tell yet! A long line of self-curses lace my thoughts.

While I sit awkwardly quiet having my internal panic-attack, Dad is silent as well, pulling the car into a parking spot across the lot of the QFC. He parks the car and pulls the emergency brake. I shiver a little. *Why doesn't he say something? Anything. Shit. He's bottling it up. Dammit, why are we so alike?*

He gets out of the car while I unbuckle the seatbelt. I consider making a bolt to the nearest bus stop and going home to crawl in my bed, hide under the sheets and slowly die. I shake my head a bit to snap out of it. That was a little over-dramatic. Okay, maybe little was an understatement. Instead, I decide to open the door and step out onto the pavement. I shut the car door quickly, take a deep, not-so-hyperventilating breath, and walk around the car to Dad. I drag my feet and keep my eyes focused on the ground, taking my sweet time. Dad decides to meet me half way and catches me in my path. I bump into him, stumbling a little. I push my glasses up the bridge of my nose, looking at him with fear in my eyes. He reaches his arms around me and pulls me into a bear-sized hug. We stand in the hug for what seems like a long time, though it is probably only about thirty seconds.

"Why didn't you tell me sooner?" he asks, squeezing me even tighter. "By now you should know I love you and support you, no matter what you do."

My throat swells and I smile, burying my face into the work shirt he has yet to change out of. I don't even care that it's dirty from hours of working in four-foot tall attics and crawling around people's basements as an electrician. I feel the tears gush from my eyes and wet the glass pressing against my eyelids from the frames of my glasses. I don't care one damn bit. All I know is that I have the love and support of the only parent I have left in this world.

🥀

A Note From Bre Klein

This event took place when I was sixteen years old. Today I am two months away from turning eighteen. Over the past few months I have discovered I'm gender fluid. I was just not happy as only one or the other. So I've tried my hand at being both. And now it's based on how I wake up feeling in the morning. Sometimes, I'm even both on the same day! It's not on a scheduled timeline. My dad, along with the rest of my family, still supports me with who I am—even if it can be a little hard to keep up with. I want other people who have issues with gender identity or who are confused about what they should do now to know that no matter what happens it will be okay. Not everyone will accept you at first. It takes time for them to adjust. A long time—be patient.

Sadly, the fact is that some people may never accept you. That is just how society works. But, you have to be true to yourself and do what makes YOU happy, not what will make another person accept you. You will find out who your real friends are, and who in your family really means something to you. It can be extremely difficult, especially with family, but you just need to push through and stay strong! You can look up support websites and hotlines that deal with gender identity issues, and move on to what to do if your family members do not accept you at first. Good luck to you on your journey!

THE UNFINISHED FORT-SHIP

NEAL TINGLEY

I HEAR THE REV of the old Subaru hatchback come around the corner. My father pulls up and honks the horn twice, as usual. Seeing him brings back the fear I feel when he hits me —like he did yesterday, like he has for the past three years. Half of my life. A cold feeling rolls over me, making sweat concentrate on my face. As I stand up on the porch, I can see cluttered junk in the back of the car.

Curious enough to dare, I ask, "What is all that?"

"Supplies," he says.

"Oh, okay," I reply. I turn back to the door when his voice stops me.

"Come around to the back of the house when you're ready," he says. He speaks sharply, enough to catch me off guard, causing me to miss the next concrete step up to the door. *Ready for what?* I think to myself.

"Okay, I wi—" My word gets cut off by the slam of his car trunk. After I shut the big green door to the house, I run the possibilities of what he wants with me through my mind. Maybe he is fixing the bathroom or some other section of the house. My father is a construction worker and he fiddles with things around the house all the time, but he usually tells me to get out of the way. He never does anything with me normally, and I can't think of a reason he would want to now. I remember the door to the master bedroom and its squeaky hinges. No, that wouldn't take more than a power tool and some WD-40. I live in an antique house in Federal Way, a great house that was paid for from the balance of money between my mother and father.

I devour the PB&J left on the counter for me by my mother, still considering the possibilities. I decide that he might have something planned for Easter, only a few days away. I pussyfoot past my mother's room, suspecting that this may be a surprise for everyone but me. I shuffle down the stairs and through the laundry room's sliding glass door leading out to our ground-level patio. Father is standing on the far right corner of our lawn wearing sunglasses. He is sorting paint, wood, and other ceramics. The day is hot and I can't help but feel excited about whatever this project is, even though I fear it too.

He never does anything with me, I think. *Ever.* I feel uneasy as I ask, "What is all this for? Is it for Easter? Or me?"

He shoots me a quizzical look. "I thought I told your mom to tell you," he says as he reaches his paint-splattered hand for me. I flinch. *Here it comes—he is going to hit me.* But instead he says, "We are building a fort," and reaches past me until he grasps the power drill on top of the tool box behind me. He explains this in a kind voice I have never heard before.

My eyes light up. *Maybe I have the wrong impression of Father. I would adore building a fort with Father so much. Or maybe this is some devilish trick, a master trick of all tricks.* Fear washes over me again as he waves his big, callused hand. "Come, Son," he smiles a normal smile. This is so unlike him; something seems out of place, like a crooked tooth on a beautiful queen. I can't help but follow him with excitement. I soon forget the thought about this being a trick as we work our way into the blueprints. He throws a 13' by 24' floorboard onto the ground.

"What color do you think you want?" he asks. "Ahhh, don't worry about it," he adds before I can respond. "We will get to the color at the end. Let's just get this thing standing!" The enthusiasm in my father's voice fascinates me. It feels unreal.

I can't believe it when the first wall comes up. We are actually doing this. I feel the leftover cement drying on my right hand. "Better get that washed off, son," he says kindly.

"Yeah, I will dad," I say. I stand there for a minute to soak in this moment.

The decorations of the first wall are structured to look professional and they actually do. The green patterns on the marble tiles seemed to line up together as they are laid upon the bare surface of wood, only now to be separated with the pasty substance of cement. Even the window is lightly covered with a red tint to give a better interior layout of contrast.

"Are you doing okay son?" my father asks, looking through me like he is looking for something behind me.

"Yeah!" I reply happily, but I don't feel how I sound when I speak to him. *Is this really happening?* I let the hammer fall onto the head of the nail, joining the next wall. *Maybe it is, or maybe I'm really still in my bed.* I watch the hammer free fall, watching the space between the face of the iron hammer and my flesh become smaller. Contact is made and an excruciating pain fades in and out of my hand. I hold back the tears and even the scream crawling up my throat. I don't want Dad to see me cry; it might make him mad.

But my father catches on to the disaster. "Hold on, I will go get the medical supplies," he says as he walks away to the house. I am left there, thinking that building the fort may be done for the day because of my injury. I cry.

I wait for a long time and still there is no sign of Father. I sit against the only solid wall of the fort, letting my injured hand wander the cool grass. The sun finally slips behind the trees and darkness falls. I walk, head down in shame, to the house. I am wondering where my father is and why he left our project. I don't see him in his usual spot on the balcony. I think that maybe he just forgot about me, which would not be a surprise. I see my mother in the antique-color tiled kitchen and walk over to her.

"Where's dad?" I ask. But she does not reply, not even a pause in business on her part. "Mom?" I'm worried now.

But as I come close to the point of breaking she turns around and says, "Let's fix that finger. You wouldn't want it to get infected now would you?"

"Okay," I reply. She speaks sweetly and calmly like everything is okay. That's how my mother always makes me feel. She has never reached a hand out to harm me. She's never even verbally abused me. She bandages my finger and then tells me to get off to bed because of the time.

I do as she says and go upstairs to my room. She follows behind me.

"Goodnight my sweet son," she says. "Sleep tight and don't let the bed bugs bite." There is a different smile on her face; I can't explain it to myself. This whole day has been so weird.

"Mom?" I say before she turns off the light.

"Yes honey?" she replies.

"Where's Dad?" I stare at her, letting my question soak in.

She hesitates before replying. "Well, your father, he's not here anymore." She speaks in a straight, solid tone. "He did bad things to your sister, and now he is in jail."

I can't believe what I'm hearing, *He's gone?*

"But what about the fort?" My voice chokes and my eyes swell up. "Will he be back to finish the fort?"

My mother pauses and walks over to the side of my bed. She is just as hurt as

I am, I can see it in her glossy brown eyes. As she hugs me so tightly I can barely breathe, my world drops and I wonder what it actually means to have no father.

"No," she says softly. "He won't be back."

❧

A Note From Neal Tingley

To this day, I have not seen my father and have never pushed further than considering talking to him. I still live in the perplexity of my own life, but I am happily pushing forward toward happiness. I hope these stories let you accept yourself for the beauty that you are. I am now seventeen, on track and working hard to fulfill my dreams. As for future plans, I want to explore as many fields as possible before choosing my career.

WHO DO I THINK I AM?

TEBRA DRAPER

"**H**EY LOSER," Wade said jokingly as he motioned for me to follow him. "Don't forget the pipe!"

"Oh yeah! Right, almost forgot ... Duh," I replied, laughing at my forgetfulness.

"In all partial seriousness though, Tebra, I am genuinely concerned about your early Alzheimer's."

This was an ongoing joke my two best friends, Wade and Patricia, had about me. I had a terrible memory, even for a stoner. Of course I didn't have Alzheimer's. I was only fifteen.

I went into our tent and dug through the piles of clothes, sleeping bags, and other random things we really didn't need. Eventually, I found my pipe at the bottom of the pile.

Cool! I thought, and hurried to zip up the tent so that no unfriendly insects would enter. I struggled to put on my Van's slip-on skater shoes. These were my favorites. I wore them everyday rain or shine; the black and white checkered look seemed very stylish to me. I thought they went with almost every outfit.

"Come on Dufus, hurry up!" Wade laughed.

"Jeez Louis-iana," I exclaimed. "Be patient, for crying out loud! You aren't the one who has been stuck in a hellhole for sixty days." *Butthead,* I thought.

The hellhole I was referring to was the inpatient rehabilitation treatment center where I had spent the last two months. This was only my fourth day out, but it felt like the first. We had been plotting this camping trip for several weeks through letter writing. Letters were what the other girls and I lived and prayed for every week. We would bite our nails every Monday morning, hoping to get a letter back from our friends and family. If no letter came, we were devastated.

The anticipation of being here with the flowing river next to our tent had been all I thought about while I was stuck in treatment. The anticipation had been bubbling and boiling inside me for too long. Finally, I was free to smoke some weed and get my drink on with my friends.

I moseyed my way over to Wade and Patricia, who were standing about a hundred feet away from our tent in the woods. We didn't want to be too close to the campsite—especially in the daytime—because we could possibly blow our cover. This property was owned by Patricia's grandparents and it was crucial that they did not find out about our activities.

"Here you go Tebs," Wade said. "You should take greens, you deserve it!"

"Taking greens" is the term for taking the first hit off a bowl of weed because it is the greenest when it is first loaded —no burns or chars.

Yeah! I thought. *I do deserve this. I've waited so long and I'm finally getting the pay-off for it.* Before treatment I had been stoned every day for three years.

Wade then loaded the rather plump, jade-shaded bud into the bowl piece of my pipe. He handed it to me with a sincere smile, excited to see me hit it. I could already tell this cannabis was potent just from the smell that carried past my nose as I brought it up to my face.

I ignited the lighter. *Finally! This is going to be so awesome to get high again.* I could feel the anticipation smothering me, but it was also making me more anxious.

I thought I had forgotten what weed tasted like. Marijuana always has a lingering scent of dank that is followed by the intoxicating aftertaste of herbal, but I had been away from my "other best friend" for so long that the familiar taste in my palette was fading.

For the next half hour or so, Wade and I passed the pipe back and forth to each other, loading bowl after bowl. Patricia didn't smoke weed, but she was cool with us smoking around her. It was obvious to Wade and me that she was more into her alcohol anyway.

Not far into the bowl, I realized that something about this high felt different from ones I had experienced before. An odd sensation began creeping up on me right after we started drinking and a strong buzz from the beer hit me. I thought it might be from getting cross-faded (smoking and drinking at the same time). But besides feeling funny, I was exuberantly happy to be sipping on Pabst Blue Ribbon, my favorite beer.

My blurry red eyes glanced over to Patricia for some sort of comfort, attempting to reconnect with reality and reassure myself that everything was fine. But as I gazed upon her, that creepy feeling grew even stronger inside me.

Then I heard it. A voice screaming bloody murder. The feeling was like hearing a car accident just outside a bedroom window. I turned to look but saw nothing. This voice sounded like my own, but the words it was using were ones I would never say.

"What do you think you are doing smoking weed and drinking beer in this stupid tent with these stupid people!?" it howled from inside my head.

What on earth was that?

"Weed is stupid! She's stupid! He's stupid! You're stupid! You just wasted sixty days of your life in that hole for nothing?" it chastised me.

Whoa! What the fuck is going on? My inebriated mind raced in little fast-paced circles. I knew I couldn't figure out what it was right then, so I tried to summon the strength to make the voice go away. All I wanted to do was get high and enjoy myself. I figured that wasn't too much to ask. I was leading myself to think I was having some sort of panic attack.

"Uhhm, Patricia," I said softly to her. "I feel really weird dude ... " I was trying to express what was happening to me in a way she could understand. I wanted her to just get it, and to tell me everything was fine.

"Oh my god, Tebra! Are you seriously sick already?" she hissed. She had a rude personality, but it really came out when she drank. I hated Patricia's way of being mean and sour. "My friend" was simply unpleasant to be around most of the time.

"Well I don't know, kind of; I'm not really sure what's happening, actually," I said, then waited for the voice to slam in again.

I really didn't want to share this odd experience I was having. I thought they would be angry at me. I thought it would hurt their feelings, because honestly it was hurting mine.

I had never felt this way about my friends before; these people were my life, my night and day. We used to hang out every day, just doing whatever we felt like. We planned to be friends forever.

"Hey Wade, you should load another bowl, yeah?" I asked, thinking that would help calm me down.

"A-ight," he replied. After he loaded the pipe, again he insisted I be the one to take the first toke.

As I inhaled the smoke from the pipe, I started reflecting on my life.

Throughout my childhood and early teen years I had struggled to grasp success and meaning. Before I made this friendship with Patricia and Wade, I had no one. I was always cast out for being different. And because of my ADHD, I was lacking skills in math, which made me really insecure about myself. My fifth grade teacher didn't even believe in me. No one really noticed the "Special Ed Tomboy" who had no friends. But when I found Patricia and Wade, I felt noticed and appreciated for the first time. The funny thing was, now I actually had an excuse to spend the money my dad was always giving me. He told me it was to entertain and take care of myself throughout the day. I was more than pleased to spend my money with them and they were happy to enjoy all the weed and alcohol my dad's money provided.

"Hello!!! Anyone in there?!!!" Patricia said. They had been trying to get my attention because it was my turn to hit the pipe again.

"Oh shit. My bad. Just spacing off. Sorry," I answered. I then became determined to fight the voice. I decided to just block it out and try to think about having a good time. I wasn't going to allow myself to be absorbed by the voice's power. I literally tried to argue with my own mind. It couldn't be anyone else that was screaming inside my head, but I was baffled that I was actually doing this.

NO! I told myself. *These are your best friends, they love you and you love them. Weed is good! You like weed!*

Silence. No reply from the strange voice.

"Well, if you are actually sick, you have to go inside the house and sleep in there. I can't have you puking in my tent, Tebra," Patricia stated after she noticed I wasn't responding to them again.

GOD, I despised it when my friends said my name in this way. I felt like they were talking down to me, that they thought they were cooler because they were older and wiser. This was infuriating. Who did they think they were talking to me this way? My keepers?

"No! I'm fine, alright?" I said, trying to claim my power back. "I don't want to stay in the house okay?" I knew that if I got up to go inside the house, I would be sick.

"I felt weird, but I'm okay now. I think I might go to bed, though." I then remembered to add, "Hey, please don't have sex while I'm in here, okay?"

"Psh!" They both scoffed at my plea. "Why would we do that? " Patricia added.

"Well, you have to ask the big questions, right?" I returned. I sure was asking myself some big questions.

"Night, Tebra," Wade said. "Pussy," he added with a whisper.

"Night, Wade. Douche," I replied with a not-so-genuine laugh. "Goodnight, Patricia," I said.

"Yup," she managed as she took another swig of beer.

Well sweet dreams to you, too, I thought.

As I was drifting off to sleep, I remembered what Wade had written to me in a letter that I received when I first arrived at treatment. "Hey man! I know they are going to push a lot of thoughts and ideas onto you, but for the sake of your sanity DO NOT let them brainwash you."

"Psh," I had laughed at this idea.

"I am only going to leave with the same stuff I came here with," I wrote back. "Don't worry, I will be the same Tebra when I return."

But as I lay in my sleeping bag, without any voices yelling at me from inside my head, I wasn't so sure. Maybe I shouldn't have been so worried about the treatment center brainwashing me. Maybe I had been brainwashed all along.

Or maybe I was just really stoned.

❧

A Note From Tebra Draper

"Let things be good, not bad. Let things be good, not bad. Let things be good, not bad."

This is the chant I would repeat to myself every night while I was a patient at Fresh Start, the all-girls rehabilitation center. I still call it out to this day whenever I feel alone, scared, or just unsure about myself and what I'm doing with my life. For the longest time, this made the bad times in life seem a little brighter and helped me to look for the light in the darkness. Fortunately, I hardly need to use this chant anymore.

I am very grateful to have learned from people who see potential in others when they are lacking. They are the most wonderful, helpful people in the world. They are the ones who change lives, one kid at a time. I want to be this kind of person, because people like this made all the difference for me. The people I am referring to are the teachers at Scriber Lake High School.

For those out there who hear the voice, don't be afraid to listen to it. It could help you in life, even if you don't want to listen. I decided to listen, and now I'm on an amazing path to my future as a teacher. I love learning and I love children. I hope to be making many differences for others in the classroom.

HIGHWAY FROM HIM

MIRANDA ESAU

WHEN YOU THINK OF THE DEVIL, what is it you see? I see a four hundred pound flannel-wearing man, a retired sheriff of seventeen years and someone who took my power, stole my soul and said I didn't matter. His name is Rick and he is my stepdad.

I remember that day I arrived home from the seventh grade. My mom's car was gone so I figured no one was home. I opened the door and entered the living room. It looked like a tornado had hit. Broken dishes were scattered everywhere. The recliner chair was upside down. My eyes locked on our white sofa, which was now splattered with what looked like red wine.

Just then I heard a rustle in the back room. I figured it must be my sister, Dan.

"Dan," I called out quickly. "Are you there?"

There was no response. I froze. Did I just walk in on a burglar? A debate went off in my mind. Do I run? Do I call for help? I decided to call for help and flew to the phone in the kitchen, trying to shut out the panic washing over me. As I reached for the phone, I saw the medicine bag on the counter. It was Rick's bag. The bag that held his pot. The bag he was never without.

I frantically started punching my mom's number into the phone. *Hurry,* my mind urged. *HURRY!*

Before I could finish I felt him behind me, ripping the phone from my hand. "You little fucking brat! What are you doing?" Rick's voice thundered.

Miranda. Get OUT OF HERE! the voice inside of me yelled. I broke free of his grasp and started rushing toward the slider door in front of me. I only made it a step before I felt him pushing me to the ground. I crawled around the island that separated the kitchen from the living room. Then I was back on my feet, focusing on the front door. Before I could reach the doorknob, I felt him grabbing me again. He slammed me against the wall so hard my head and body punched through the plaster.

My head was spinning and I felt my body fall to the floor. For a second everything went dark. Looking up, I saw only his faint shadow and white dots across my vision.

This is it, I thought, preparing for another hit.

I looked again and saw him disappear into a back room. *Where did he go? It can't be over. He's coming back to kill you. YOU HAVE TO GET UP.* I crawled toward the overturned recliner and tried to use it as a prop to pull myself up.

I saw him coming back toward me. Then I heard the front door open, saw my mom and heard her scream. "What did you do to my baby? Get away from my baby!"

Rick was screaming too but Mom ignored him. She was bending beside me, her arms around me. Rick went silent. He knew he had gone too far. Without saying a word, he stepped out of the house and shut the door behind him.

I expected him to be back as soon as I returned home from school the next afternoon. But when I got home, it was just Mom, sitting on the stained white sofa.

"Mom?" I asked nervously. "Where is he?"

I stood at the door, bracing myself. Mom walked over to where I stood and I saw relief on her face.

"Don't worry, baby. He's gone," she said.

A flood of emotions consumed me. My brain went into overload. First it was relief. *I'll never see him again. There is a God.* Then fear quickly took over again. *Will he be back? Why after so long did he finally go?*

I wanted to believe my mom, but it was hard. I started lying in bed each night, ready to go into action. I would sleep with my phone tucked beneath my pillow with one hand on it, so I was ready to call for help if he showed up. Some nights I would finally start to doze off, beginning to think about good things again, when the slightest noise would startle me and bring me back into my paranoia. My mind would start racing, flooding with scenarios of what he would do and what would happen if he were to show up.

Weeks passed and there was no sign of Rick. I began to relax. If he hadn't come back by now, then why would he ever? I began returning to my "normal" life. I started sleeping again and was finally able to really smile.

❦

The day started out great. I got up to find a delicious breakfast Mom had made waiting for me on the table: eggs, bacon, even apple juice, my favorite. School was better than ever. The guy I liked finally admitted that he felt the same. I was caught up in all of my classes and the school dance was only two days away. Nothing could bring me down. We had been assigned a new project in woodshop so I knew a trip to Craft Star for paint and other supplies was needed. I LOVED going to Craft Star.

My after-school agenda was set: I would hang out with my friends (including the boy I liked), then meet my mom at Craft Star at six to get what I needed so I could start on my project that evening.

The day went perfectly. School was great, my friends and I had fun hanging out, and while at Craft Star, Mom decided to let me pick up a few extra craft supplies. On the way home she casually mentioned Rick.

Mom hadn't spoken his name in a while and just hearing it brought back my fears and anxiety. But her news was good. "He hasn't bothered me since he left," she said in a calm, relaxed tone.

"Good, Mom. Because I swear, if he comes around again, shit's going to get real!" I nearly shouted the words so she knew that I was serious. I was expecting to hear her chastise me for swearing, but she didn't. She understood.

"No worries, baby. He's gone."

I trusted her. She was my mom. She had to be right.

She started singing to a song on the radio. But the minute we pulled into the driveway, she stopped. I looked at her face. Her mouth turned down and her eyes were locked on our house.

"What's wrong, Mom?" I asked, trying to keep my voice steady.

"Oh, nothing. The porch light is off and I could have sworn that when I left, I made sure to leave it on."

I thought I detected worry in her voice, but I couldn't tell if she was scared or just confused. My mind started racing. *Him. It can't be. He hasn't even bothered her. There's no way he could be here.*

"Mom," I said, hearing the tremble in my voice. "Could it be him?" I was unable to say his name out loud.

"No," she answered, her tone firm. "I drove by Mike's house, where he is staying, and his truck was there. That's his only way to get around. So there's no way he's here."

"Okay, Momma. Just checking." I tried to sound confident. I didn't want her to see me scared.

I felt the tension in the air as soon as I stepped out of the car. My gut told me something was wrong, but I pushed the feeling aside and made my way toward the house, clutching my Craft Star bag in one hand, my keys in the other. Midway to the door, I stopped to make sure Mom was close behind me.

As I put my Tinkerbell key into the deadbolt, I fought the urge to turn around and run. The urge was stronger than it had ever been before. But I couldn't figure out why.

It's okay. You are just being paranoid, I told myself.

I turned the key and pushed the door open. That's when I saw Him. He was a shadow in the dark, sitting on the recliner with the moonlight cast behind him. I froze as I watched him rise and hurl toward me.

"Is there a problem here?" His voice was evil, menacing. He finished his sentence by cocking his gun and putting it to my face.

I knew that sound. It meant RUN!

🥀

April 1, 2012—Five Years Later

"Will you come down and see us?" The text from my mom reads as if it's an everyday thing. "Room 112 Baby Girl. Can't wait to see you."

I'm now living with my dad in Edmonds. My mom and Rick are living in Montana. I rarely see them anymore, and I miss my mom more than anything.

A jumble of thoughts—fear, anger, curiosity—rush through my mind as I realize what I've just been asked to do. But it is too late to turn back now. I have already sent a text back to her and have agreed to the visit. Knowing how much she hurts everyday with me not there, I set all my emotions and hesitation aside and head out the door. It's not until I lock my front door to leave that I really start to think about all the different things that could happen. *He could hit me. He could hurt me. He could pull a gun on me.* Jumping into my car, I blast the stereo, hoping to drown out my unwanted thoughts.

I arrive at the hotel twenty minutes later, park and take a deep breath. *This is the right thing to do,* I reassure myself. I continue to reassure myself as I walk down the hall. *You can do this. He can no longer hurt you. Just breathe.*

I stop in front of a door with the numbers 112. I knock on the door. Silence. I wait, wondering why there is any delay. I start to walk away. But then I hear his voice.

"Where are you going?" he says, stopping me in my tracks. I turn around, expecting to see my fear staring back at me. Instead I see a man who is weak, brittle and broken. He looks as though he can barely stand.

"Oh hi, I thought you guys weren't ... well never mind, hello," I say, forcing myself to smile. I follow him into the room and see what I expect. My mother is in bed, almost lifeless. I try to play it cool.

"Hi Momma, I've missed you so much!" I exclaim.

"Wow Bug, nice hooker tights!" she chuckles.

"They're not hooker tights. But thanks Mom." I try to act like her words don't hurt. I change the subject. "How are you, Momma?"

When she speaks, it's as if it takes all her power. "I'm okay, sick but being strong," she says, her words interrupted by a string of coughs. "What's up with you, Baby Girl?"

"Oh, you know. The usual. Dad's an ass, but I'm doing great in school," I say.

Sitting next to her makes my heart break. The woman I once knew is gone. I remember when I used to look up to her and think she was the most beautiful woman I had ever seen. Now she is who I promise myself I will never become. Continuing the small talk, I realize my stepdad has left. This is my chance.

"Mom," I say quietly. "What's going on? You're sick. He's drunk. You promised." I begin to choke up thinking about every promise she's ever broken.

But she plays stupid, as though she has no idea what I'm talking about. "Miranda, what are you talking about?"

"No Mom, stop. You know." We are interrupted by the door knob turning. I quickly change the subject as he walks through the door followed by my grandma, Susan.

"Well hello darling," she says. "Don't you look amazing!"

I realize I want to get this evening going so I can be done.

"Hungry?" I say.

"What a great idea, M. Mom, are you ready?" Rick asks. I look over at her, expecting her to get up. But she doesn't. She calls me over and immediately I know what she's going to say. "Love, I don't feel very well, but you guys go." I feel sick to my stomach. *What am I doing here? I'm only here to see her and now I'm stuck with him.*

I force myself to stay calm. "Okay, Mom, we'll be back."

I kiss her on the forehead and hug her like I never have before. I know this may be the last time I see her and the thought kills me. Walking out the door I fight back tears. *In only a little while I'll be back home in Edmonds,* I assure myself.

We walk into the Chinese restaurant and I head toward a table. Rick grabs my arm and directs me toward the bar. "Um ... Rick I can't go in there," I say.

"No, it's fine, yes you can," he answers.

"Okay, if you say so." *God he's unbelievable. He can't even get away from alcohol for an hour.* I lose my appetite sitting across from him. It makes me sick to hear him talk about how much I mean to him and Mom and how proud they are of me when his words are all just bullshit. Half of the time he is rambling, not even making sense with the sentences he speaks. It makes me want to stand up and walk out. But out of respect for my grandma, I stay. I wonder how she does it. How can she sit across from her alcoholic, drug-addicted, abusive, asshole son and keep her cool? If she can do it, so can I.

"Hey man, keep your eyes off my daughter unless you want your knee caps broken!" Ricks words snap me out of my thoughts. I ignore his threat to the man smiling at me. *Gross!* Hearing him call me his daughter disgusts me. It makes me sick to my stomach—almost making my recently consumed Chinese food come up. I concentrate on finishing my food so I can leave. After a few minutes I glance back at Rick. I want to look away, but something stops me. Time freezes and forces me to look deeper. He's still the revolting four hundred pound mass he was before, but now he wheezes when he talks and every few words are interrupted by hacking coughs. Those eyes that once scared me are now sunken into the back of his head—the result of years of drug abuse. I am no longer that scared twelve-year-old girl. I'm seventeen now and I'm strong.

This is the moment I realize I am free. I am no longer afraid of him. The man that was once my every fear, my biggest nightmare, is now nothing but a weak human being.

I pass the next hour just shutting out the sounds around me. Every once in a while I notice another drink being delivered to the table. Rick's drunk as usual. I don't care. It's almost over.

When we are finally done, I feel as if the world has been lifted off my shoulders. I cannot wait to get back to the room to tell my mom goodbye and that I love her so I can get the hell out of there. Walking back to the room, Rick remarks on how beautiful I am. I have never been so insulted by someone's compliment. I try to ignore him and continue to the room. I find my mother still lying in bed. My arrival has awakened her.

"Sorry Momma. Just coming to say goodbye, then I'm outta here."

"Oh, alright Baby Girl. I'm sorry again for not going. It's just I feel so sick and .."

I stop her. "It's okay Momma, I understand."

Although it hurts that I never see her, it's almost better that way. Looking at my mom as an addict and knowing she is killing herself is one of the hardest things I have ever done.

"I love you Mom. Please take care of yourself and don't forget I'll always be your bug."

I feel the tears building and know the flood is coming unless I get out. I give her one last hug.

"Please say goodbye to Rick and thank him," she whispers in my ear.

It takes everything I have to keep from exploding, from screaming at her for telling me to thank him. Instead I agree and give her one last kiss.

I head toward the door. "Thank you for dinner, and take care of Mom. Please." My words sound like a request but in my head I'm begging him to take care of her.

"I will, always have. Be good M, we love you," he says, his eyes glossy and glazed over. He reaches to hand me the one thing he has always held over my head: money. As badly as I need it and would love to have it, I know denying it is my ticket to freedom.

I look him directly in the eye and stare hard.

"No," I say. "You keep it. I'm done with this game." I grab the door handle and look back one last time.

"Goodbye Mom, I love you," I say again and walk out the door.

A Note From Miranda Esau

Seventeen years old. A junior in high school. Five foot eight and … a REDHEAD.

This is me, Miranda J. Esau, the girl I have grown to love. Growing up I went through the same things many people do. The teasing and the constant put-downs unfortunately got the best of me. My pen and paper became my get away—the only thing I thought would ever understand me, and it couldn't even talk back. I was afraid to be judged or to put myself out there.

But there comes a time when you have to jump and be ready for the impact, no matter what may happen. That is what made me write this story. I want to let other teens know that you can get past anything and that you are never alone. There is always someone, somewhere, who is willing to listen, but you have to be willing to make yourself vulnerable and open.

I have always lived by the saying "This too shall pass," and to this day I constantly remind myself of it. No matter how bad you feel one day, every day is another new start and only you have the power to change it. So don't dwell on the bad, the ugly or the evil but instead, stand up, claim your power and know that you can't have the sunny days without the rainy ones. I hope reading my story has let you realize that by opening up and sharing your story with others you can find self-relief and really move forward. The day you do this will be the day when someone asks you "Are you okay?" and you can honestly look at them and say "Yes. Are you?"

My motto: "Embrace the haters!" <3

THE DAY MY WORLD STOPPED

AMELIA DAWN DAHLEN

MY MOM IS CHOOSING A VIDEO GAME over me.

The muffled voices turn into full throttle when I open my door. As I step into the hall the screams get louder. It's not like it is anything new; this has been going on for a few months. The fights just get louder the more they come, ever since Mom has been spending all of her time on the computer.

"You don't understand. They are my parents and they need me!" my mom screams as she sits on the couch with a sour look.

She is trying her hardest to convince my father that she needs to go to Vegas to take care of her parents. But I know that's not really what this fight is about. Mom spends hours playing Slingo and chatting with her "friends" from different states, and the story about her parents is a cover. I try to speak to her so that she will notice me, but she just stares straight ahead through her thick-rimmed wire glasses.

In the last week I had noticed her getting sucked into her new world more and more. One time I approached her just to talk, but she was engrossed in the game.

"What?" she barked at me when I sat down.

"Can't I just sit and talk with you?" I replied, feeling like I was talking to myself. I recognized this person in front of me but I did not know where she had gone.

"I'm busy Amelia, what do you fucking want?" she snapped without even looking away from the computer.

My stomach fell.

"Mom what the fuck is wrong with you? Why can't I just sit here and talk with you?" I screamed back. I thought that maybe I could get her attention if I talked to her in this way.

She grudgingly pulled her eyes away from the screen.

"Amelia, I said I'm busy. I'm your mother and you need to listen to me. Now go to your room or do something other than be in here." I had gotten up and walked away as she turned back to her computer. She didn't want me. She didn't want me near her, interrupting her fantasy world.

Now my dad is experiencing the same thing; he is scared, too.

"Damn it, Donna," he pleads. "Your parents are grown adults and you have a life and a family here that needs you!"

Really what we all want is her attention, for her to come back into our family. We don't know how to approach her in her new world.

My mom stares straight ahead, arms crossed, looking at him as if he is the most annoying person on the planet. My dad storms out of the house, taking the screen door off the hinges with him. Surprisingly, she follows. My dad has never been the gentle type. Though only five foot nine, he's strong, with scars on his face and the grease-stained hands of a mechanic.

I sit on the couch for what seems like ten hours while my parents stay outside and yell back and forth like two cats in the wild. This fight is worse, much worse, than the rest. It seems to me that every word is being vomited out. When the yelling is done, Dad leaves on a walk. He's livid. As I'm listening, the fear grips me that he may never return.

My mom comes back into the house, slams the door and paces back and forth with a red face and clenched fists.

Then she stops, looks at me and says, "Amelia, get your shit. We're leaving."

I sit and stare at the mirror on the wall above the fireplace, unable to move. *Did my ears just hear what I think they did? She wants me to come with her? All of a sudden she is talking to ME? She hasn't paid attention to me in weeks.*

"Amelia get the fuck up and get your shit!" she yells again as she comes stomping back into the living room.

I snap out of my zone of disbelief. I am so desperate to be wanted by her that I find myself jumping up from the couch, running to my room and shoving whatever I can into a small bag.

Mom goes back into the living room and tells my oldest brother calmly, "TJ, I'm leaving and Amelia's coming with me."

"What are you talking about?" he asks, surprised.

"Your father is mean and cold and no one in this house respects me anymore," she barks. "I'm not happy and I haven't been in a long time." She's standing over my brother with her fists still clenched.

"Mom, just calm down. I'm sure everything will be ok," TJ says, trying his hardest to calm her.

But my mom hates being told what to do, and she hates being questioned.

"Amelia let's go!" she yells, way too loudly.

"Ok I'm right here Mom, no need to yell. I want to say bye to Dad. Can't we please wait a minute?"

"No Amelia. We need to leave now," Mom says as she yanks my bag out from my hand and heads for the door.

I follow her to the car. Her face is still flushed and she's gripping the steering wheel as if it might fall off. She pulls out of the driveway like a crazy person. I know exactly where we are going the moment we get in the car—to her sister's house. My drug-addicted aunt only contacts us when she needs money or drugs. But Mom doesn't have many people, anyone really besides my aunt, who she can call at nine o-clock at night and say she needs to come over. While my mom yells her curses to the sky, I sit in my seat and cry, watching the street lamps fly by. I ask myself why I'm with her when she doesn't even care about me.

"Why?" I finally ask.

"What do you mean, why?" she replies.

"Why are you doing this? Dad loves you. We all do. We need you, Mama. Please don't let this happen."

"I can't do it, Milly, I just can't. The way he treats me, it's not right. He's rude and mean. I don't ever want to be around him," she says with more and more rage. The more she talks, the more upset she gets and the faster she drives. The next thing I know we are speeding down the highway.

I know that any word from me is going to send her racing faster toward the edge, but I can't help myself.

"You're a liar," I say. "He's not like that. He loves you and does whatever he can for you. Why can't you see that? He would never do anything to hurt us, ever. I know it. Why would you say those things?"

"You don't understand. You're just too young. When you're my age it will all make sense, I promise." She's annoyed. She won't listen to anyone.

It takes all I have not to open the van door and jump out of the car. Hearing her talk about my dad that way makes me want to be anywhere but sitting next to her. I sure as hell would have jumped out the very second she started talking this way about him if I knew I wouldn't be hurt.

But that's not how things work. I do what I do best and keep quiet the rest of the drive to my aunt's house.

When we arrive, my mother jumps out of the car and runs to her sister who is now standing on her porch, arms crossed, chain smoking, waiting for my mother's embrace. She stops smoking long enough to wave for me to come inside. Glued to the car seat I sit and watch as my aunt Mel, with her stringy black hair and sunken eyes, fades away into the house with my mom. I think about my dad. I wonder if he knows where I am or even what's going on. All the emotions I have inside me, every little thing I've been holding in, explodes out of me in one swift, loud scream.

Five minutes pass before I decide to go in, dragging my feet the whole way. As I reach the front door, before I can even think, Mel opens it.

"Missy Dew!" Mel screams as she pulls me into her embrace. "How you doing, Sweet Pea?" I start to pull away from this woman who I haven't seen in months.

I want to say, "Well, if you must know my mother pretty much just kidnapped me, told me she was never coming home and that my dad is a horrible person. Now I'm standing in front of you, a woman who I only really see when she needs money or pills from my mother. So, please, tell me how you think I'm doing right now."

But "I'm fine" is all that comes out.

As I step into her house the smell of Jack Daniels and cigarettes fills my nose. There is never much furniture in her house. "Why have so many things if you never know where you're going to be the next year?" is Mel's motto.

Bella the cat is my only friend when I'm here. Bella is really the only thing she has had longer than a year, other than her out-of-work husband who is asleep on the only couch. I take a seat next to Bella in the hallway as my hands start to shake and my head gets numb. I realize I will not be going home tonight. I can feel my body aching as I cradle over into the fetal position.

I lay for what seems like an hour on the cold, hardwood floors with Bella in my arms before my mother and Mel come back into the house, laughing. I'm mad. My world is falling apart, and they are laughing. My mom wanted me to get in the car with her, but she has left me on the floor, alone.

I try my hardest to compose myself before they see me, but my eyes cannot hide the hurt that I feel inside. As I turn the corner, Mel's now-awake husband is the first to notice me.

"What's wrong, Little Shit?" he barks as he takes a long drink of his beer.

"Nothing, I'm fine." I try my hardest not to be rude.

"Amelia Dawn Dahlen! How dare you talk to him like that! He's your uncle," Mom says.

"No, he isn't really my uncle and you know that. But you're my mother and right now all I really want is to talk to you," I shout as I stomp off into our room for the night.

It's an hour before my mother tumbles into our room. I'm sitting on the bed reading and I can tell she's been drinking. But still I need to talk to her.

"Mom. We need to talk," I say, exhausted, as she climbs into bed. *Why am I here? I'm thinking. What is the point?*

"Oh, what do you want now? Just go to sleep," she says as she lays her head down.

"No. I can't just go to sleep. I need to talk to you," I say, pleading.

"Okay, then talk. I'm listening," she says in a voice that means anything but that.

"I'm not staying with you and I hope you know that. I need to go home and I need to be with Dad and the boys right now. I'm all they have. I know you'll be fine without me. But Dad, he needs me." As I speak these words, I realize this may be one of the last conversations I have with my mother.

"Then go," is the last thing she mutters before passing out for the night.

I leave the room and head back to what seems like the only safe place I have tonight: the tiny hallway. I realize that my life is never going to be the same. I stare into the blackness of the house, letting my eyes adjust to the darkness. I'm uncomfortable on the floor, so I walk to the living room. It seems as if the creeks in the floor get louder with every step I take. Not like it matters. Mel and her husband are long passed out by now. I climb onto the old couch and lay my head on the only pillow, though it feels like a boulder under my head.

I am completely alone.

❧

A Note From Amelia Dawn Dahlen

It's been a year and a half now since my mom walked out of my life. In that short time I have come to realize that everything we go through in life is just another story to tell, another experience we have to look back on, whether it be good or bad. My mother leaving was not one of the best experiences in my life but it has made me who I am today: a strong, outspoken, confident, and all-around fun-loving person. Now only three months away from graduating, I am happy, healthy, and completely content with everything in my life. The saying "It's always darkest before the dawn" is true. I've been through the dark. Now it's time for my dawn.

BE[LIE]VE

JASMINE GIFFORD

W E WERE SITTING TOGETHER on the cold, hard ground under the West Seattle Bridge. It was three in the morning. We were looking mindlessly at the black sky and the busy traffic. The yellow and red lights that flashed from the cars, streetlights, and bright signs in windows, were all vivid blurs of color around us. The city ignored us like he had been ignoring me. I wanted to talk, but there was a frozen silence between us that I didn't have the nerve to interrupt. I was shivering even under his coat, which was wrapped much more tightly around me than his arms were.

We were trying to get through the night after an evening of drinking with our two street-kid friends; one of them was my best friend, the other was his best friend. They had ended up wandering off together somewhere and we were stranded. No place to stay and nowhere to go.

It was March, a little after a year and a half of us being on and off. Earlier in the day we had met up at the downtown Seattle library. He knew I would be there, since his best friend told him. I didn't know he would, since my best friend didn't tell me. It was the first time since late December that we had seen each other—the first time since we had broken up for the second time. It was also the first time even speaking to each other since I couldn't ever get ahold of him. He could have gotten ahold of me—but I didn't like to think about that.

All four of us met in the bright red hallway of the library. My stomach dropped to my knees and my heart rate skyrocketed as soon as I saw him.

"So, I'm sorry I haven't messaged you back on MySpace or anything ... I've been really busy. I was in jail for a while," he said, flashing me an apologetic smile.

"It's cool," I replied casually, without making eye contact.

"I missed you. How've you been?" he asked, trying to pull me away from our friends.

"Fine."

It was tense and awkward between him and me for the first little while, but it didn't take long for us to start smiling and kissing and holding hands like we hadn't fallen apart months before, and months before that, and months before that.

"Let's go to our spot," our friends said, referring to the area in West Seattle where they spent their time drinking and getting high on whatever they could find. Now that he and I were together again after so long, we didn't want to go with them. But they dragged us along on a few different busses until we got to the bottom of the bridge, across the street from a little diner and auto shop. It was partially hidden; we could see out but no one could see us. It wasn't a pretty sight. There was gravel all around us; beer cans, cigarette butts, and even a couple of Playboy magazines were scattered around. Our friends chugged back their twelve percent alcohol, orange-flavored Tilts and eventually left.

Despite feeling uncomfortable where I was, I was with the guy I loved and I was giggly and happy like I used to be with him. He kept telling me how much he had missed me and thought about me, and we were both glad when we were finally alone.

"Finally," he seductively whispered with a kiss on my neck ...

A few hours later, we were still there. The mood had changed now that we were cold and lost. He absentmindedly rubbed the small of my back and I laid my head on his chest, like we were back together. But we weren't.

All night I wanted to clarify what was left between us, but I didn't want to ruin the day we had. I wanted to be able to fall asleep with him and not worry, but it was impossible. Something inside me made me break the silence.

"Do you still love me?" I asked. The question slipped out before I realized I was even going to ask it. I was immediately overtaken with regret and intense anticipation. My stomach clenched so tightly that I couldn't breathe. As soon I said it, all I could do was hold my last breath and wait.

He hesitated. Finally, he answered in a small, hesitant voice. "I still care about you ... "

He kept looking out into the night as his hand made small circles on my back. It took a moment for his words to sink in and when they did, the knot in my stomach got even tighter. My stomach hurt, my head hurt, my throat burned, my face felt hot against the cold air. I could feel the tears well up, even though I tried so hard to stop them. *I still care about you*. Not love. Care.

Care.

Care.

Care.

I hated him for saying it. I hated myself because I already knew. I knew it was all a waste. I knew he didn't love me. I mostly hated myself because I was unlovable.

It was actually hearing it. His voice actually speaking those words out loud, making it real and true. His hesitation was what made it even worse. He *thought* about what he was going to say. His decision was to tell the truth and there was nothing I could do. What did I want? Did I want him to tell the truth, or did I just want him to lie again? It was what our whole relationship was built on. He always lied to me, like an unspoken agreement—one that I had never agreed to.

A year and half worth of lies, broken promises, insults and accusations, they all burned inside me at that moment. He had unleashed everything I kept hidden deep down somewhere, never before letting them out in front of him. Alone, I had spent countless late nights crying as I waited for a call or a text from him—no matter what it might say. Of course, they hardly ever came. For a year and a half I was constantly waiting for him, and I was constantly disappointed.

Like the day after we broke up the first time. He hit on the girl he knew I hated right in front of me and fed her Ecstasy—pill after pill. Or like the time we agreed to meet at the Lynnwood Transit Center one day at three o'clock. I waited from two-thirty to four-thirty, just wandering around with a friend, not telling her who I was waiting for and making her tell me stories to pass the time and calm my nerves. The *next day* he was there, stumbling drunk with his friends and slurring his words in a ridiculous apology. Or like all the times I wished he would spend the day with me but I was forced instead to settle for letting him sneak in through my window late at night and leave as soon as he was satisfied.

I still care about you ... the words echoed in my head over and over like a curse. Time just kept creeping by slowly while my heart raced like the cars around us. He sat there acting like nothing had happened.

I began slowly inching away from him. When I was a few feet away on the hard, cold ground, I buried my face in my knees. I silently scolded myself for acting like such a child, but I wanted him to feel the distance between us that I felt. The wind kept blowing my hair around but for once I let it be. I had no energy. I knew it didn't matter how I looked to him anymore anyway. I knew I looked pathetic, about to cry under a bridge over something I had already known. If he loved me, everything would be different. If someone loves you, you wouldn't ever have to question it. Soon he was beside me and began what I knew (and secretly hoped) he was going to do. "Jasmine ... I'm sorry ... don't be upset ... I didn't mean it ... God what was I thinking? Of course I love you ... you just caught me off guard ... I love you."

He tried to get me to turn around and face him but I shut my eyes tightly and covered my ears with my hands. I didn't want to listen to his lies, but mostly it was just to show him I wouldn't let him console me. Trying to get me to open up to him, he started rambling about how he never did anything right and that all he ever did was fuck everything up, and that, of course, *he loved me.*

"Come here. Don't cry, babe. Please. I only came to Seattle this morning to see you. I love you. I don't know why I said that."

I didn't say anything back. I pretended I was ignoring him and focused on the faint warmth of his sweatshirt around me, hating myself again for having to wear it. I wanted to rip it off and throw it at him, but I also needed to keep it on, to feel like a part of him—even if it was just a sweatshirt—was with me, keeping me safe and warm.

His begging for me to look at him disgusted me but also made me feel wanted, which was becoming so rare. I let the messed up, broken part of me indulge in his insistence that I look at him, loving the attention and his soft assertiveness.

"Please," he said, running his hand through my hair and down my back. Affection was becoming rare, too; I didn't want him to stop, but I couldn't let him know that. I stayed still and silent.

Frustrated, he sighed and leaned over to grab his stuff. "Do you want me to leave?"

He would *leave me*? I came back out of my sea of inner contradictions, the ocean of love and hate thrashing around inside me. I looked up and remembered that I was under a fucking bridge in Seattle, miles away from home. He was about to *leave* me here? At three in the morning? In the freezing cold? I couldn't believe it. Actually, I could. It made me laugh a little inside, thinking how I let myself get this low. *What's wrong with me?*

"I don't care," I replied. My tone was colder and stronger than I anticipated.

He tied his shoes a little tighter and got up to leave. *No, I don't want to be alone. I need him.*

I needed him for many different reasons, not just because of where I was. I knew our friends were probably down the street—but I just wanted *him* there. I tried to justify it by remembering that there were no busses and my phone was dead and what if my friends were further away now? But I really just needed him with me. *I should have forgiven him ...*

"Can I have my coat please?" He said it like a statement, not a question. Impatient and demanding, but still, somehow, in a quiet, apologetic way. Instantly tears flooded down my face and I started to unzip it. I pulled the security off me and threw it at him like I had wanted to do. Cold air stung my exposed skin.

But I needed his coat to stay on me, and I needed his arms around me—even if they were loose and not as comforting as they once were.

So I faced him.

"Wait. Don't leave."

I had to depend on him to stay with me, like always. I had to pretend that I wasn't crying, like always. I had to pretend that I believed him, like always. We had to say "I love you," and "I love you too," and I tried my best to convince myself that it was true. Like always.

A Note From Jasmine Gifford

I hope that everyone who has been in this position knows now how much of a waste it is to let yourself be stuck in a dead-end relationship, especially if all you're getting out of it is just getting hurt. I wish I could say it was all worth it and that it was a learning experience, but almost three years of my life feel wasted, and all I learned was that you can't spend your time crying over someone who would never cry over you. On a lighter note, I'm eighteen now and about to graduate, ready for college, and ready to be independent.

HELP YOURSELF

CHARLIE MAGDALENA

"I CANNOT HELP YOU if you don't tell me what's wrong."

I just look at her with a blank stare. Her face is flushed red, she is frustrated—as she should be, I guess. I mean, as a mother, what are you supposed to do when your child is lethargic to everything that is going on around her and she has only just reached the age of seven?

I felt a swift fist connect with my jaw. I was knocked to the ground and everything went black for a split second. I opened my eyes to see many pairs of short fumbling legs and light-up sketchers shoes in a tight circle around me. My attackers were in only the first grade, like me.

"Why don't you get up? Where's your mommy at, Freak?" A boy gestured at me in a mocking tone. All the others tagged along and laughed with him. They began to chant and repeat after him.

"Freak! Freak! Freak!"

I was laying on my side, making no effort to move into the fetal position. I could care less about the beating these kids were giving me. The bruises would fade. The part I was stuck on was the mental scarring, because I knew when the sun rose again tomorrow, my mind would still be here, lying in the road. I felt a warm stream of blood slither down my bottom lip and drip to the pavement. I tried to focus on the metallic taste in my mouth so I didn't have to concentrate on the boy punching me in the ribs or the girl kicking me in the shins. I laid there on the pavement lost in my own mind. *Why don't you just do away with yourself? It won't make a difference to anyone's tomorrow. Just lay here until they leave. Just lay here until you die. Everything would be so much easier if you would just die.*

It was like having someone in my head telling me all these terrible things about myself. If I couldn't escape ridicule from kids my age, from my family, and even from myself, where could I go from there? Where could I find solace when I had no one?

I peered around the corner of my brother's bedroom door to observe the screaming match in the living area. I was five years old. The argument was growing louder and more violent with every word. This was nowhere near the first time this has happened. Like a tick. Every time he came home, if he came home at all, she exploded.

"You know what? I'm done. I'm just done with this," she screamed as she shoved a stiff finger into my father's face. "We can't keep doing this anymore."

Once again I peered my head around the door to see them both locked in a silent, angry stare, eyes hard as stone. This time the fight felt different—disconnected and almost sacrilegious.

"You can't keep doing this to your kids," she continued, more quietly. "You know they love you more than anyone ever could, and you disrespected that unconditional love. You disrespected my love. We can't take this anymore. I won't let your selfish actions control the way this house is run any longer. You are never here. Your drinking is way out of control. I just don't know what to do anymore. I'm lost."

"Fine, then," my father responded, knowing his actions had been everything she'd said. "If that's the way you feel. Just remember that you chose both of us not being here for the kids then, not me."

Then I heard his heavy steel-toed boots head down the carpeted hallway to the master bedroom. I shut the door quickly. I heard the frightening slams of drawers and wardrobe doors. I wasn't scared because of the loudness of the slamming, but because he had communicated to me that he was leaving to work again in about another week or so. I didn't want him to leave, and he knew so he always warned me before he did. I hated it when he left. When he was around, I felt like at least one person in the house wanted to spend time with me.

I heard him return from the bedroom, duffle bag in hand. I tried to cut him off midway down the hall and only got out a squeak of disapproval before he shuffled me to the side and headed for the front door. My mother stood her ground until she heard his pickup rev its engine and peel out of the driveway.

I rushed to the window to see his truck pull away like it had many times before, except this time it felt different. Panicked emotion swallowed me whole as I turned to see my mother collapsed and sobbing heavily on the couch. I ran to my bed and covered myself in the puffiest of comforters and pillows. I hid myself from the world under all my blankets. I rocked back and forth, sobbing as hard as a five-year-old could sob. I cried myself to sleep that night.

❧

My mother and I were heading home from a day in the first grade. It was a sunny, pretty easy-going day. I had managed to get by without being pestered by anyone and was looking forward to hanging out with my best friend. My best friend had the most beautiful silky black hair and the brightest green eyes. She was always easy going and kind, and never rejected anyone. She accepted everyone as her friend, no matter what. She didn't judge me and I didn't judge her. We never even exchanged any words, but it's not like we could anyway.

As we turned down the long gravel driveway to our little yellow three-bedroom house, I began jumping up and down in my seat. I couldn't unbuckle my seatbelt fast enough. I ran to the front of the house to check around the rose garden first. She always liked to scratch herself on the thorns and play with the ladybugs covering the rosebushes. I saw no sign of her, so I ran to the backyard and all around the shed and the swing set. I even checked inside my tree house. Nothing. *Well,* I thought to myself, *she usually shows up around dinner time if she isn't here now.*

I heard my mother call my name and I knew she wanted me to come inside for my bath. I could hear the warm water running from just outside the backdoor. I took off my shoes and my jacket and made my way to the washroom. I stripped to my birthday suit and hopped in the tub. My mother began to wash my hair with sweet smelling green apple shampoo.

"Hey Mom," I asked. "Where is Blackie at?"

She paused. "I actually need to talk to you about that," she said finally. I noted the change in her voice.

"What about her?" My voice wobbled as the fear built up in my system. I was afraid for what she was about to tell me.

"We ... we had put her down, baby. The cancer was spreading so fast and she was in pain. You saw her stomach falling out of her skin ... She wanted out. There wasn't anything more we could do for her. She was suffering." Mom was still and spoke as if on autopilot.

I didn't know how to react. I was overwhelmed with dread. I felt vomit leave my mouth as I babbled wildly on and on about her being gone. My best friend was dead. And she was never coming back. My only form of stability and support had left this world. Now what was I going to do?

I had never felt more alone than in that moment.

❧

"I cannot help you if you don't tell me what's wrong," my mother says.

I just look at her with a blank stare on my face. I do not have the words to tell her the truth. In this moment the only thought going through my mind is, *Even if you tried your hardest, you couldn't help me. Because like you've always said, "In the end, the only one who can help you is yourself."*

I look her in the eye and say, "I'm okay, Mom ... I'm okay."

❧

A Note From Charlie Magdalena

"... on a mote of dust, suspended in a sunbeam." Carl Sagan

I lived with depression for a long time. But I knew I wanted out. I was tired of lying in my bed every day and sobbing to the point of passing out. I remember being in bed on a sunny warm day in April and looking at the white blinds reflecting off of the natural light. I never open my blinds, I thought to myself. I stared at them for a moment before crawling out of bed and walking to the window. I remember thinking that it must feel nice to soak up warmth from the sun, and as I opened my blinds, the sunlight hit me dead in the eyes. All of a sudden I realized that I had been looking at everything all wrong. It hit me that all of my negative thoughts were ones I was controlling. That's the day I started realizing that I was the only one who let myself dwell on issues that bothered me. That's when I started to figure out that all I really needed to be happy was myself.

It has been awhile now since I have had problems with depression and/or suicidal thoughts. I have now almost completed my senior year of high school and plan to attend a university in the fall of 2012 with twelve thousand dollars in accumulative grants thus far! I plan to further my education in fine arts, chemistry and self-sufficiency. Wish me luck! And always remember: You don't need to read a self-help book to help yourself.

STICKS AND STONES

KAYLA KINNARD

I HEAR GLASSES BEING THROWN against the walls. The loud noise of my father's rage wakes me from my sleep. I am nine years old and it is the night of New Year's Eve. The clock reads 11:00 p.m.

I rip the covers off my sweating body and walk to my bedroom door. My heart feels like it is going to rip out of my chest and I don't know if I feel anger or fear. My adrenaline is through the roof, but it takes a good ten minutes to convince myself to open the door. I hear my parents arguing, but I can't make out the words. I eventually turn the knob and walk out toward the living room.

I can see the destruction that my father has caused. This is a daily occurrence in my house. The walls are dripping and stained with the remains of filled glass mugs that have been smashed against the walls. Glass lies in shards across the floor. I see my mother standing in the living room and my father standing in the kitchen. I don't really know what the fight is about, but I am sure it is unimportant. It always is.

"Stop being such an instigator," my mother demands as she picks up shards of glass. "You just can't leave it alone! You always have to have the last word." She doesn't look at my father when she talks to him.

Because this happens every day, I am able to block it out fairly well. But tonight something feels different. I decide to sit on the couch and wait for everything to calm down. I start thinking about my situation. I think about where I'm going to end up and what my future looks like. I begin to wonder if my exposure to abuse will make me predetermined to repeat it. I wonder if it's my fault. Though my outer appearance shows nothing more than a child, I know that I am different from most kids my age.

My mother moves to the living room to pick up more broken glass and objects that have been thrown onto the floor. My dad is known for clearing tables in anger. They proceed with their shouting match across the house.

"Look at what you did! Now I have to clean all of this shit up," my mother hisses toward him.

"Shut the fuck up, you fat fucking cunt!" my dad screams at her as he fills his glass with ice at the refrigerator.

I see my mother head toward the kitchen and move past him to the trashcan to discard a dustpan filled with broken glass. My father continues to scream, corners her and lowers his six-foot body so he is pressed chest to chest against my mother's five-foot frame. She stares at him as he yells, but the contact is broken when she heads back into the living room. She decides to taunt him a little. She walks toward our kitchen table that is filled with an assortment of trash. She picks up a half-empty soda can and chucks it at his head. The look on his face is a mix of embarrassment and rage. He doesn't speak a single word, but his face reddens and his stance changes to a military puffed-up posture.

"Fuck you!" she laughs as the contents of the can drip down the wall behind him.

I enjoy seeing my mother hurt my father. Sometimes I fantasize about coming home to his murdered body or about murdering him myself. Other times I think about the terrifying possibility of coming home to my murdered mother. I am aware that this is a disturbing thought for a young girl to have. I don't think my friends think about these things.

When she turns her back to him, my father opens up a drawer and pulls out a knife. I can't see his face, but his body language shows his rage. I watch as he flies toward her and pushes her against a wall. He tries pushing the knife into her chest, but she grips the handle with all of her might and doesn't let go. I feel outside of my body, like I'm watching someone else's mother get pinned against the wall right in front of me. I am without emotion; I cannot register this scene. I don't think his intention is to stab her. But with my father, I know that anything is possible.

I snap back into my body in time to see my mother's saddened eyes looking at me. "Close your eyes, Kayla," she says calmly, in a nurturing way.

I don't close my eyes. I don't even cry. I just sit and watch. Before I have time to react, my father loosens his grip, turns and throws the knife on the seat next to me. He then takes my mother by the hair and throws her beside me. I feel the weight of her body landing, which causes the room to shake.

Every time I see this violence between my parents, I freeze. At times I have asked my mom if I should call the police, but she tells me that they will both go to jail. Or that the police won't do anything about it. She always tells me that it's okay. If I say this to my dad during the abuse when we are alone, he hides all the phones.

I start to think about all of the times my father has abused me. Like the day he went looking for me when I was outside playing with a friend. It was mid-July and only the middle of the day, but he insisted that I was supposed to be inside and that I was past curfew. When we arrived home, I knew I was in big trouble. He pressed his face against mine and started screaming. I began to cry hysterically and slumped down to the floor. I couldn't muster up a word, even though I wanted to defend myself. He demanded that I stand up, but my legs felt like Jell-O and I was too afraid. He grabbed me by my hair and dragged me from the living room all the way to my bedroom and closed the door. That was one of the most humiliating experiences of my life. I didn't feel like a human being and I certainly didn't feel like his daughter. Instead I felt like a disgusting dog. I sat on my bed and cried while brushing my hair repeatedly.

Along with the physical abuse, I thought about the emotional abuse I dealt with every day. I thought about how stupid, ugly, fat and worthless I was because I heard it, not only from my classmates but from my own father. I was always afraid of asking him for help on schoolwork because, if I didn't understand something, he would ridicule me. He would stand over me and repeatedly hit or flick the side of my head while calling me names like "retard" or "stupid."

"What's so hard about learning how to read a fucking clock? Dipshit!" He would yell, flicking the side of my head.

The words replayed over and over in my head. I honestly thought at times that I had a mental disability and that no one had wanted to tell me.

�️

While sitting on that couch, I think about all the pain my father has caused my mother and me. I am always afraid to stand up for myself; instead of growing into my own, I am growing into a weak person who is incapable of being strong. I am sick of hearing the muffled screams of my father choking my mother, the emotional and physical abuse. I am sick of being a prisoner in my own home.

Just like my mother, I snap. I leap off of the couch toward my father. I throw my body at him and begin pulling and clawing at any piece of flesh I can touch. His face shows a look of shock as I begin to spew hateful words.

"I wish you would just die. I fucking hate you!" I yell as I try to hold back tears.

My father says nothing, but places his hands on my shoulders and pushes me. My mother starts to approach me as my father heads to their bedroom. She tries to calm me down by telling me it's okay, and assuring me that she is okay, too.

"It's definitely not okay," I want to scream. Instead I say nothing. She raises her arms in a gesture to hug me, but I move out of her reach. I am not only mad at my father, I am mad at her. Why doesn't she just kick him out? Why is she putting me through this?

After the mess is fully cleaned up, my mother and I sit on my bedroom floor, huddled in front of my tiny television screen. Both of us are waiting for the New Year and a resolution.

I sit on the floor eating tacos—the New Year's Eve dinner my mother always makes—trying to shut the evening out of my mind.

"Ten. Nine. Eight. Seven" ... the announcer's voice booms from the TV.

I think about the year ahead, wishing, hoping that it will be different.

"Four. Three. Two. One," the announcer continues. Cheers erupt in the background. "Happy New Year!"

❦

A Note From Kayla Kinnard

It took a couple of years for me to realize that I have no control over anyone's life but my own. It's still a battle sometimes to look in the mirror and see myself and not my father. But I've finally realized that I can either dwell in the past and give my father power, or move on and take my power back. And I'm choosing to take my power back.

I am now a graduating senior at Scriber Lake High School. I enjoy spending time with my friends, reading and cooking. I am currently a certified nursing assistant and plan to attend Bastyr University to become a midwife. My biggest goal is to have a rewarding career where I can help others. My hope is that my experiences can help another person who has gone through a similar experience. I want people to know that they have the power to decide who they are and where their lives are headed, not anyone else.

SUICIDE MISSION

JEANETTE FIGUEROA

MY MOTHER WAS LYING IN THE HOSPITAL, dying of liver failure, and it was my fault.

I felt a knot in my throat as I looked out the window and watched my sister leave the house with *them* to visit her. I didn't even bother to ask if I could come; I hated that family and they hated me.

My mom had known them back in Mexico when she was a teenager. A year earlier—before my mom got ill —they all decided that it was a good idea to move in together to save money. But it wasn't a good idea. Their daughter, Alma, and I started to get into trouble together —boys, drugs, shoplifting and gangs. Alma's mother blamed it all on me and was trying to isolate me, "the bad influence," from her and my little sister.

I wanted to go to the hospital. I loved my mother. And I just wanted to tell her I was sorry. For everything.

I thought I was alone in the house, but I realized I wasn't when I heard someone talking on the phone. At first I thought it was Alma, but it was actually Alma's mother, Maricela.

"It's all her fault," she was saying angrily in Spanish. "Jeanette always gave her headaches and stomach aches. She's a bad daughter and has turned out worse than I ever thought. She doesn't care if her mother is sick. If she did, she wouldn't be doing what she's doing. If anything happens to her mother it will be that rebel daughter's fault. Juana doesn't deserve this."

At first, Maricela and I had loved each other. She had been like my second mom. When she found out about the incident with the guys, though, she turned completely against me. She regarded her daughter as the perfect girl —a goody good who wouldn't do anything behind her back. If she only knew.

Of course, it's always my fault, I thought. She had been blaming me for every bad thing, and Alma was skilled at letting her see only what she wanted her to see. I was always straight up with my mom; if I was bad I owned up to it.

My mom was going through a hard time. Months before a doctor gave her a prescription that made her turn yellow, both her skin and even her eyes. Friends would ask her why and she would say that it was side effects, that everything was normal. But now she was in the hospital. Really sick.

As I heard Maricela talk on the phone it felt like all my blood was boiling inside my body. I wanted to open the door and slap the shit out of her because she was lying. I would have slapped her, but that would have made everything worse and I didn't need more problems.

Instead I went straight to my room, threw myself on my bed and burst into tears. It was the only thing I could do—cry and cry until my eyes dried up. I cried because my mom was all I had since my parents' split. I felt so lonely. I pictured her lying right next to me, saying comforting words. "It's okay, everything is going to be alright." I imagined her familiar gesture of brushing back my hair with her hand.

I was scared, I was mad, and I was angry at the world. I was tired of people judging me, acting like they were perfect and like they knew me. They had no idea how I felt and what I was going through.

The next thing I knew I was in the bathroom, not able to talk anymore because I'd been crying so hard. Maybe it was my fault. I slumped down on the floor and remembered what had happened just a week before. When I had visited my mom at the hospital I had acted like a complete stupid little bitch to her. That night I was lying down in a small extra bed next to her reading a magazine. My mom asked me if I could read out loud to her so she could fall asleep. I told her, "No. You know I don't like reading out loud."

"Oh, okay," she had answered in a sad voice.

Later, around three o'clock in the morning, my mom whispered to me, "Jeanette? Can you help me get up? I need to go to the bathroom."

"Don't you see I'm sleeping?" I answered in a frustrated voice. "I'm tired. You can do it yourself."

"You think I would be asking for your help if I could do it myself?" she had responded, upset. Those words really affected me. I felt like shit. My mom didn't deserve the way I was treating her. "OK, hold on," I said. I got up and pulled her up by her arms.

Just the memory of how ill she had looked that night made me realize that maybe it was my fault. I wanted to die. I knew my friend's dad had sleeping pills to help him with his back pain, so I grabbed them from the counter and stared at them. Lying on the cold floor that was still wet from my sister's shower, I opened the container and looked at the pills. I decided I would use them for my soul's pain.

I prayed. I knew that God existed and that praying was the only way to communicate with him.

"God, please help me, I can't handle this anymore. Everything is my fault, I don't deserve to live. I don't want to live like this. It's my fault my mom is in the hospital dying. But why her? Please, I will give my life if you help her get better," I promised as I cried and begged. That's how my prayer ended. I was willing to sacrifice my life for her.

I went through the bathroom drawers and found a razor knife. I grabbed it and started cutting myself. "L, O, V, E," I cut into my arm. *Something I will never have*, I thought to myself. I watched the blood fall down my hand. As I cut myself I thought about all the things that had made my life miserable. I felt no pain. The next thing I needed to do was take those pills.

As I swallowed the first one I heard the doorbell ring. *Who could this be? I* thought. I decided to ignore it, but then it rang again. Something made me pull myself up off of the floor. Maybe it had something to do with my mom.

I opened it to find a little girl with brownish hair, light skin and big, dark brown eyes standing in the doorway. With a sweet yet frightened voice, she asked, "Is Abi home?"

I realized she was frightened of me. My eyes were red and swollen. My face was red like a tomato, and my make-up was smeared all down my face. My hair was hanging in a tangled mess.

"No," I responded with a serious voice. "She's not."

The girl didn't even bother to say goodbye. She just turned around and ran off. I understood. I'm sure she thought she had seen a dead person. I headed back to the bathroom, but I was in shock.

I sat and stared quietly, not crying. Then I thought, *Maybe this was a sign from God*. So many things started flooding my mind. *My sister. If my mom dies, I'm the only person she'd have left.*" Abi was only ten and needed me to look out for her. Once more I started crying.

"How can I be so stupid?" I said out loud.

I hadn't been thinking. I felt selfish for only seeing my own pain and no one else's.

I stood, looked at myself in the mirror, and wiped the tears from my eyes. I cleaned up my smeared make-up and washed my face with refreshing cold water.

"I have to be strong," I said to the girl in the mirror. "I know I can do it, not just for me."

❦

A Note From Jeanette Figueroa

I am now seventeen years old and I'm considered a nice and respectful teenager. I have learned many things from my life experiences. I like fighting for what I think is right, and dislike people that judge the outside but never look more deeply into others. I now consider life important and I fight for those I love. Taking the easy way is sometimes the worst way. I thank God every day that I'm alive and surrounded by love from my real family and friends. My mom survived her illness and now lives a normal life.

We are never alone; there is always someone that is going to be there for us, either down here on earth or up in the sky.

LIKE FATHER, UNLIKE DAUGHTER

STEPHANIE TANGEDAHL

"**T**HEY'RE GONNA RECOGNIZE THE CAR," Marilyn said, the panic apparent in her voice.

Marilyn was my dad's girlfriend; she was always on edge or bitching about something. She and my dad were talking in hushed voices in the kitchen. My boyfriend, Trevor, and I could hear them from the back deck.

"No they won't. It's a little old lady car," my dad reassured her.

"It's a green Taurus. They're going to recognize it. Plus, we were there not too long ago."

"Quit your worryin'. Let's just go," my dad replied in a tone that indicated he was through talking.

Trevor and I were sharing a roll-your-own cigarette full of pipe tobacco when Marilyn and my dad came through the open sliding glass door.

"We gotta run to Lynnwood real quick. We'll be back in an hour," my dad said.

"Can Trevor and I go?" I asked. I had a feeling I knew why they were going to Lynnwood. It had to be meth.

"No, you guys just hang out here, we'll be back shortly," he said casually.

"Fine," I agreed.

I knew I shouldn't argue. There was no way they were taking us with them. They filled their coffee mugs full of beer like usual and hurried out the front door. Trevor and I went inside and sat on the couch flipping through channels on TV.

"Where're they going?" Trevor asked. I was pretty sure he knew, only I wasn't one hundred percent sure myself.

"They're on and off with meth; well, my dad is anyway. I'm not totally sure about Marilyn though," I told him.

The whole situation was bothering me. Trevor and I had only been dating for a few months and my dad was already this comfortable around him. Plus, Trevor told me that he'd been into meth once before, which made it even worse considering he liked my tweaker dad.

"Your dad kind of looks like the type of dude who would be into that," Trevor observed. My dad was tall and muscular with the slightest beer belly. He had long, stringy hair that he combed over his head to cover his bald spot. Years of tattoos, souvenirs from prison, were scattered over his arms and across his chest.

I shrugged. I got off of the couch and walked to the slider. I wanted to shift the subject and make something to eat. I went outside to the pantry and got a can of clam chowder and then went to the stove to heat it up. I stood there thinking about how my dad had been like a stranger when we picked him up after four years in prison when I was nine. My sisters and I were all in the back seat of my mom's caravan. She kept telling us that Daddy was coming home. We knew our dad was in a place called "prison," but we didn't know what that meant.

The night we picked him up it was pitch black outside. The only light came from the few street lamps, which tinted everything slightly orange.

"There's your daddy!" my mom exclaimed, motioning toward a man with shoulder-length hair walking toward the van. "Okay girls, what are you waiting for? Go say hi to Daddy."

I was extremely nervous. Who was this man that I knew when I was younger? I was hesitant getting out of the car. I didn't know what I should say or do. *Should I call him Daddy?* He was like a complete stranger; we were meeting him all over again. Once out of the car, Mom already had her arms wrapped around Dad. My sisters and I slowly approached them.

"Well hi guys," he said with a smile. He bent over with his hands resting on his knees, so he was almost at our level.

"Hi," my sisters and I replied shyly.

"You guys are so big now. I remember when you were just this big," he measured with his hand.

Once he stood up, Mom made us all have a group hug. When we got back in the van, Mom and Dad were busy talking about grown-up stuff. I was still stuck on how awkward I would feel calling him "Dad," but how equally awkward it would be if I called him "Shawn." I decided that until I felt more comfortable, I would just get his attention by saying, "Hey."

As I stirred the bubbling chowder, I realized that my dad was the root of all my problems. For three of the past eight years he had been home, I had constantly worried about him. I worried every time he drove drunk without a license. I worried about how he had a warrant out for his arrest, and about the varicose veins in his legs that could burst at any moment. And I worried about his lack of self-love. He always said, "Dad's gonna die one day anyway," whenever we told him he needed to care about his health. It occurred to me at that moment, standing at the stove, that I didn't want to lose my daddy again. And here he was, out risking his freedom. And for what? A little bit of dope?

Trevor and I ate our clam chowder and sat around watching TV until Dad and Marilyn returned. As soon as the front door opened, they headed straight for their bedroom. They didn't say anything to us. They just went into their room and shut the door behind them. I went to the bathroom and heard them talking in low voices. When I came out I stood with my ear glued to the wall by their door.

"What are you doing?" Trevor mouthed. I put a finger to my lips as a signal for him to remain quiet.

"Cut it right, cut it left," I heard my dad say. His voice was muffled from behind the wall. I ran over to Trevor, who was sitting on the couch.

"He said something about cutting it right and left," I reported.

"It's probably coke," he said.

"I don't think my dad does coke. What about meth? Whatever they're doing, they're snorting. Can't you only smoke meth though?" I asked, confused.

"No, you can snort it, but it's really bad on your nose. That's why you shouldn't touch it with your bare hands," he informed me.

The way he said it made me think he just thought he knew what he was talking about. I knew that meth was a really bad drug, but I wasn't too sure if it could hurt you if you held it with your hands. Sometimes I was unsure about the things Trevor told me.

"Then it probably is, he's done it a—," I stopped when I heard them open their door. I got up and walked over to the counter where my glass of milk sat.

"Dad, is this your milk?" I asked, pretending like it wasn't mine so I could get eye contact.

"No, I don't know whose it is," he croaked, wiping his mustache. He was looking down.

"Are you sure? Because it's not mine or Trevor's." I knew I sounded like I was making it up. Not like he could tell, though; he was already spun. He looked at me and I looked him directly in the eyes. His pupils were small and quick. He turned around and headed toward the back deck for a cigarette. I followed him outside and made sure Marilyn was still in the bathroom. She always tried to butt into conversations like it was all about her. Her appearance always reminded me of a witch, wearing rings on every finger but one.

"I know why you guys went to Lynnwood," I said awkwardly as he lit his cigarette. He looked at me blankly, his mouth hanging open.

"Dad's gonna do what Dad's gonna do," he said with a shrug, dismissing me.

Just then, Trevor came out. "Wanna share a cigarette?" he asked me.

"Sure," I replied.

I handed him a cigarette and sat on one of the folding chairs in the corner on the deck. My dad and Trevor were standing five feet away, next to each other.

"I'm so jealous you get to do that," Trevor said, referencing my dad doing meth.

"Don't ever touch that shit," my dad warned him. "You be a good boy, man."

Trevor then turned and handed me the cigarette. He came over and sat next to me in the other chair. I guess he wanted to drop the conversation with my dad because he knew he wasn't getting anywhere with it.

⁂

Edmonds, Washington, 2005—seventh grade. My cousins and my aunt were over at our apartment when my dad stormed in the house like a monster. He had just swallowed an eight ball of meth, but we didn't know it. Mom was gone. Aunt Margaret said she was at the casino, but not to tell Dad because it would piss him off to no end. Little did we know.

Aunt Margaret was at the kitchen sink washing the dishes when he stomped in. The rest of us were in the living room.

"Where is she?" he demanded.

"I don't know, Shawn," Aunt Margaret answered quietly.

"You know where she is, so tell me," he said in a haunting, angry tone.

"I really don't know where she is. She just went out," she said, cowering. Aunt

Margaret looked intimidated. She was the only adult in the apartment besides my dad, so it didn't make me feel secure knowing she was afraid, too.

My dad's tone was accusing. "She's here, isn't she? She's hiding somewhere."

"No, she isn't in the apartment. The Jeep is gone; she's not here," my aunt assured him. My dad turned around.

"Shawn, I'm going to take the girls back to my place. They can spend the night and I will bring them back here tomorrow when Jennifer's home," my aunt said.

"They're not going anywhere," my dad shot back sternly.

For the first time in my life I felt afraid of my dad. I felt small and defenseless.

"Please, just let me take them for the night. It's only a night. They'll be back tomorrow," she pleaded.

"I said no!" He slammed a beer bottle on the counter.

Everyone became quiet. I got off of the futon from watching TV and walked over to the hallway facing them. I knew I had to do something about this.

"Dad, please let us go," I said. I tried with all of my heart to sound convincing. "We like staying at Aunt Margaret's house. And there's nothing to do here."

"You guys are staying here." His words were final.

There was nothing more I could say to that. He was not going to let my aunt take us back to her house. I was overcome with anger and fear. With the way he was acting, no one could predict what he would do next.

I went with my sisters and older cousin, Crystle, into our bedroom. We sat on the queen-sized bed that the three of us shared and talked. Crystle tried to comfort us while Dad was running through the house like a madman. He was picking things up and looking everywhere for my mom. The rest of the house seemed to be quieter now that Dad was here. Everyone was afraid of how he would react if any of us did anything that didn't please him.

Time passed slowly. We remained in our room, talking in low voices until Dad came in with a wooden baseball bat and a big, metal police flashlight.

"Where's your mom? I know she's in here."

"She's not here, Dad," we said, our voices shaking. I got off the bed and my sisters and Crystle all huddled together.

"Yes she is, I just saw her run in here," he yelled.

He was hallucinating. Mom was nowhere in sight.

"Dad, she's not here. We swear," we pleaded. We must not have been very convincing, because just then, he lifted the bed with my sisters and Crystle still sitting on it.

"I saw her run in here and hide under your bed," he said with a crack in his voice.

I was standing beside him in the doorway. He was kneeling on the ground with the bed still in one hand and the bat in the other.

"She's not fucking in here!" I screamed as loud as I could.

"Ooh, good one," he said smartly. He dropped the bed, stomped into his bedroom and shut the door behind him. We all tiptoed into the living room where the rest of my cousins and my aunt were. We were all quiet, careful not to wake my raging monster of a dad.

A few hours later, we were all still watching TV when my dad emerged from his bedroom. He looked around crazily and walked into the bathroom. Once he was finished, he went out the front door of our apartment without looking back. None of us had any idea where he went.

※

Dad's gonna do what Dad's gonna do. I was packing my backpack, getting ready to leave. I couldn't stop thinking about what my dad had said the previous night. *How could he say that to his own daughter? How could he be so selfish?* My bag was on the chair next to the dining room table. Marilyn was on the back deck smoking a cigarette. I said goodbye to her and looked over into my dad's room. The door was open and he was lying on his stomach on his bed. He was snorting a line.

"Hey Dad, I'm leaving," I called. He turned toward me nervously. He was covered in sweat and looked terrible.

"Huh? Okay," he said.

"Want a hug?" I asked hopefully.

"No," he answered, and went back to his line.

"Okay, love ya. Bye," I said, embarrassed.

There was a lump in my throat the size of a golf ball. I felt like shit, like my stomach was going to fall out. I was angry, sad, ashamed and embarrassed all at once. I felt like I was losing my dad again and he didn't even care.

A Note From Stephanie Tangedahl

"You do anything long enough to escape the habit of living until the escape becomes the habit."—David Ryan

As of today, my dad is off of meth. I was unsure if he was ever going to stop. Meth is something bad that many good people get into. If you know someone who has an addiction, remember that no matter what you say to him or her, they can only help themselves. As for myself, I am nineteen, graduating high school and will be going to college in the fall to become a dental hygienist. I want to make a difference in peoples' mouths.

ME, MYSELF AND YOU

LAUREN NEIN

I'M DONE. Done, done, done.

Sitting on my bed, I just want this all to end. Stop the thoughts. Pull the plug. This is it. Slice, watch the blood fill the cut and gracefully fall down my hand. Slice, not deep enough. Slice, I'm such a failure. They're all right. Well, it should all be over soon. But I wake up about an hour later pissed off that I'm still alive.

The feeling of hopelessness engulfs me. As I stare at my plain ceiling I hear their voices, which are more like hisses, replaying in my head. *Fat ass! Freak! You're better off dead!* They are right, about all of the above ...

❦

When I entered the doors of Brier Terrace Middle School, I somehow knew I wouldn't be leaving them as the girl I knew myself to be, and I was right. I was twelve years old when I attempted suicide, and when that didn't work, I found my new best friend: hurting myself.

Along with my dad losing our beloved home due to the economy and the loss of his job, I also lost my dad to crippling depression. I loved him so much. I was devastated to leave him and move in with my mother because we screamed at each other to the point where I thought our throats would bleed. On top of that, I was treated as a diseased alien at school, which meant I had no friends. I had two people to hang out with outside of school, but I knew they only did it to pity me. I didn't care though, they were still company. When I found cutting, it quickly became a consistent part of my life; I could hurt myself worse than anyone could. Sure my peers broke me down and made me hate every fiber of my being, but when I was cutting, I was the only one who got to hurt me. I was the only one who was able to carve as deep into wherever as I wanted. I was the only one who got to see me as the weak one.

Every day became a routine: wake up, fake an illness, try to sleep the depression away. And when the last one didn't work, that's when my legs became my canvas.

That's when I stared at my oversized, jiggly, disgusting and tattered thighs and cried. I couldn't help but wonder, *When would this end? When would the clouds that covered me dissolve and allow me to be a free spirit?*

🌷

Cutting became an addiction that followed me for years. But it ended when I met you. The years passed. I was fifteen and a sophomore in high school. But I was still cutting and still hopelessly depressed. At that point I had friends who had introduced me to the rave scene, and, of course ... ecstasy. A lot of it. With consistently depleted serotonin, my depression only got worse. But somehow, you still wanted to talk to me, hang out with me ... flirt with me? No, couldn't be. Who would want to flirt with ... me?

One day in late April we were on a bus to nowhere special. Your tone of voice got extremely serious. "Why do you never let me touch your shoulders?" you asked.

I laughed it off. "Because, they're my shoulders. Only people of extreme importance get to touch these bad boys."

I should have known by the look on your face that you knew something was seriously wrong. You ignored my comment and fought my dark green sleeves off my shoulders until you saw what lay beneath them: ugly scars, healing scabs and fresh, bright red cuts. You reacted in such a way that I almost felt bad for doing it. But who am I kidding? I had just met you. You would forget and we could move on. But I was so wrong.

"Call me next time if you need someone to talk to. Just please, call me," you said. Were those potential tears in your eyes? Couldn't be.

"Okay, I will." And that was that, we let the weeks pass and didn't mention that bus ride once. It was better that way.

🌷

One day after walking into my apartment, I looked around to see my bedroom — which was the living room—occupied, as usual. I stared at my bed on the living room floor and realized that I had no privacy. Nowhere to go. I felt so lost and conflicted about my life. A sudden feeling of hatred swallowed me whole. The mundane thoughts were so suffocating that I ran into the bathroom, the only place I had any sort of privacy, and locked the door behind me. I frantically searched through the cupboards, looking for something sharp enough to break through my hated skin. Something that would make the pain go away.

I ended up splitting my shaving razor in half and hacked away at my shoulders. Emotional and physical pain became one the second I sliced my shoulder. The pain was nonexistent, and for that moment in time, I felt good. Alive and full of adrenaline. I kept going, cutting until I was satisfied. When finished I took a red towel to my shoulder and pressed it hard, but the bleeding wouldn't stop. The towel became saturated and useless. I just laid limp in the bathtub, letting the blood drain down my arm into the tub. I felt a sense of panic rising throughout my body. I choked it back as long as I could until I burst into tears.

Why am I doing this to myself? Why do I hate everything? I needed help and I needed it fast.

I called you, like you told me to. The sound of your voice was soothing and full of concern, just what I needed. I followed your directions to apply pressure to the area and waited for you. When you arrived at my apartment with open arms, your embrace was something I had been waiting for, for so long. I held on to you for as long as I could, crying and choking on my own spit.

"It's okay, everything is all right," you said, moving your hands through my hair.

When I calmed down from the panic, we smoked a cigarette—or five. The silence was so comfortable that I wanted to pause that moment forever. For the first time in my life, I had found someone who cared about me, someone who wanted to be there for me of their own free will, not because they felt bad for me. However, with all of the glory in that picture-perfect moment, there was something much deeper than the joy of finding someone who cared. This was someone who I could hurt and someone who could also hurt me.

The process repeated itself several times. Cutting, getting scared, wanting you, and calling you. When I called you one night I was looking forward to hearing your voice, but I was greeted with something much uglier than what I anticipated.

"Why are you doing this? Don't you see what you're doing?!" you said to me.

I was speechless. Nothing could have prepared me for the hurt I felt right then.

"I can't fucking do this. I care about you too much to watch you destroy yourself like this!" I could hear your angry sobs and envision the tears stream down your face. The face that until now had masked the pain I had personally inflicted.

"I'm sorry," I said.

"I don't care. I told you I can't keep doing this."

"I.. I know.. I'm sorry ... "

"I can't talk to you anymore, Lauren." You broke away to regain your composure. "This is too much, it hurts too much." And then the line went dead.

Panic mode struck again, only that time I didn't have anyone to call. All I could think was, *Great! I fucked up once again, back to square one!*

I walked outside, barefoot throughout my apartment complex, wincing when I stepped on a rock but not bothering to remove it until I reached a patch of bright green grass. I collapsed into a ball on the soft grass in the darkness that was night. I felt lonelier than I ever have. Lonelier than in middle school when I had no friends and my dad was unreachable. Lonelier than when I tried to kill myself. I felt like the scum of the earth and the throbbing in my shoulder was a taunting reminder of my failure. As I lay in the grass, I clutched my phone, hoping for your call. It was that moment when you saved me from myself, even if you didn't realize it. It was that moment in time when I understood I was not walking this world alone anymore. My actions were now negatively affecting another soul that I cared about deeply.

I worked up the courage to call you and with each ring I became more nervous for your potentially angry or hurt voice to reach me at this end of the phone line. When you answered I stopped you from trying to continue where our last conversation had left off.

"Please, just listen to me. I need you to understand that I will try my hardest to stop harming myself, for you. And though I'm still depressed, though I still hate myself, I will work on finding a new outlet for my anger."

I held my breath waiting for your response, fearing that you would just laugh.

"Okay, I'm still here. Just know ... if this happens again, I won't be coming back."

❧

A Note From Lauren Nein

"It's okay to be messed up, because there are five guys who are just as messed up as you are. And if we have overcome that, you can too."—Gerard Way

The quote above is the quote that kept me going until I met "you." Knowing that there was someone else out there who had been where I was, knowing that I wasn't alone, was the most comforting thing. What I'm trying to accomplish with telling this story is to let someone, anyone, know that you are not alone. I want to tell you that it is okay to be messed up, you will overcome it and when you do, you will be stronger than you ever thought possible. Nothing will break you. And if you already know that, tell someone who doesn't.

I turned my love of My Chemical Romance into a passion for music of all sorts. It became my new outlet. Music had always been a huge part of my life thanks to my father, but after I realized I couldn't continue destroying myself, I surrendered myself to the sounds of music. I'm not going to lie to you: I'm still depressed and it's still hard, but I have so much respect for myself now that I will never let depression take me alive. And it's thanks to these hard times that I found out what my potential career will be—music therapy.

I can't stress enough how much you, whoever you may be, need to understand that you really are not alone. Anything anyone tells you about yourself does not matter. How do you see yourself? In your one life, your one chance, how do you view who you truly are? The you that only you know? That's what matters.

I'm not perfect, but this is me. And I'm still growing, still learning, and still overcoming every obstacle life throws at me.

ABOUT US

Scriber Lake is an alternative high school in the Edmonds School District, located just north of Seattle, Washington. Ours is a school of choice; some students come to Scriber as freshmen, some come seeking a second chance, and some land here for a last chance. The majority of Scriber students have felt lost in the system at some point and many find success in our program. We are a school of small classes and caring teachers who strive toward creative approaches to learning. Scriber is a family.

Marjie Bowker has been an English teacher at SLHS for seven years. Ingrid Ricks is the author of *Hippie Boy: A Girl's Story* and has been working with Marjie and her students since January 2012. The conception, design and writing (and editing, editing, editing) for this book were accomplished during a four-day mini-course. The fourteen remarkable students involved were 100% committed to the vision of this project from day one; otherwise, it could not have happened. We owe a special thank you to Scriber Lake Principal Kathy Clift and the Edmonds School District for putting their full support behind this project.

THE STORY BEHIND THE STORIES

A NOTE FROM INGRID RICKS

Even before publishing my coming-of-age memoir, *Hippie Boy: A Girl's Story,* I knew I wanted to share my story with at-risk women and teens. I envisioned using it as a tool to help them face down their challenges by finding their voice and claiming their inner power.

I wasn't sure what form it would take. I just knew that this was the overall message of my story and a message that I was passionate about getting out into the universe. Then, in early December, high school English teacher Marjie Bowker contacted me. She told me that a mutual friend had given her my book to read. Her next words were an early Christmas gift.

"*Hippie Boy* is the book I've always wanted for my students," she said. "Do you want to form an author partnership with my school?"

Neither of us was sure what an author partnership even meant. But we both knew we wanted to figure it out. So on a whim, we started brainstorming and Marjie was soon crafting a curriculum that used *Hippie Boy* as both a reading and writing guide to help her students claim their power by sharing their own stories in a narrative scene format.

Our month-long curriculum kicked off January 4th. And magic has been happening ever since. Marjie's students have dealt with the kind of heartache and tragedy that most of us can't even fathom. They've experienced gang life and drug overdoses, and have lost loved ones to prison, murder and suicide. Some have been shuffled from house to house without ever having a safe place to call home. Some have been battered and abused and neglected by those who were supposed to protect them.

Using a variety of interactive class discussions and writing exercises as their guide, the students spent the month of January working to bring their own stories to life. On February 1st, we hosted an in-class celebration and all-day reading so the students could share their life scenes. They were so charged up by the power they had found within themselves that nine of them stayed after school for nearly three hours to share their stories with a producer from a local public radio station.

Marjie and I realized that we had hit on something powerful and had to keep going. So we decided to offer an intensive four-day mini-course in April, with the intention of helping those students who were interested and committed to turn their draft life scenes into finished stories and publish them in a group story collection that would carry their powerful words out into the universe.

We Are Absolutely Not Okay is the end result of that intensive mini-course. But we're convinced it is just the beginning of an incredible life journey for the amazing students involved. Having experienced the enormous validation and healing power of personal storytelling, Marjie and I plan to continue our author/school partnership with the message that through writing and sharing their stories, teens can find their voice and claim their power.

CPSIA information can be obtained at www.ICGtesting.com
Printed in the USA
BVOW08s1103070913

330536BV00001B/36/P